innocent

Copyright © 2011 John Simmons
Cover design: OpalWorks Pte Ltd

First published in 2006 by Cyan Communications Limited
This edition published in 2011 by Marshall Cavendish Business
An imprint of Marshall Cavendish International

PO Box 65829, London EC1P 1NY, United Kingdom
info@marshallcavendish.co.uk

and

1 New Industrial Road, Singapore 536196
genrefsales@sg.marshallcavendish.com
www.marshallcavendish.com/genref

Other Marshall Cavendish offices: Marshall Cavendish Corporation. 99 White Plains Road, Tarrytown NY 10591-9001, USA • Marshall Cavendish International (Thailand) Co Ltd. 253 Asoke, 12th Flr, Sukhumvit 21 Road, Klongtoey Nua, Wattana, Bangkok 10110, Thailand • Marshall Cavendish (Malaysia) Sdn Bhd. Times Subang, Lot 46, Subang Hi-Tech Industrial Park, Batu Tiga, 40000 Shah Alam, Selangor Darul Ehsan, Malaysia

Marshall Cavendish is a trademark of Times Publishing Limited

The right of John Simmons to be identified as the author of this work has been asserted by him in accordance with the Copyright, Designs and Patents Act 1988.

A CIP record for this book is available from the British Library

ISBN 978-981-4351-28-7

Printed and bound in Great Britain by
TJ International Ltd, Padstow, Cornwall

John Simmons

innocent

**The inside story of Innocent
told from the outside**

Marshall Cavendish
Business

OTHER BOOKS BY JOHN SIMMONS

In the Great Brand Stories series:

*My Sister's a Barista: How They Made Starbucks
a Home Away from Home* (Cyan, 2004)

Winning Together: The Story of the Arsenal Brand
(with Matt Simmons, Cyan, 2006)

The Writer's Materials trilogy:

We, Me, Them & It: How to Write Powerfully for Business
(Cyan/Marshall Cavendish, 2006)

*The Invisible Grail: How Brands Can Use Words
to Engage with Audiences* (Cyan/Marshall Cavendish, 2006)

Dark Angels: How Writing Releases Creativity at Work (Cyan, 2004)

As an editor and contributor:

The Economist Guide to Brands and Branding (co-edited with Rita
Clifton, Profile Books/Bloomberg Press, 2003; revised edition 2008)

26 Letters: Illuminating the Alphabet (co-edited with Freda Sack
and Tim Rich, Cyan, 2004)

From Here to Here: Stories Inspired by London's Circle Line
(co-edited with Neil Taylor, Tim Rich and Tom Lynham, Cyan, 2005)

Common Ground: Around Britain in 30 Writers (co-edited with
Rob Williams and Tim Rich, Cyan/Marshall Cavendish, 2006)

The Bard & Co: Shakespeare's Role in Modern Business
(co-edited with Jim Davies and Rob Williams, Cyan, 2007)

Books on Writing

26 Ways of Looking at a Blackberry (A&C Black, 2009)

Room 121: A Masterclass in Writing and Business Communication
(with Jamie Jauncey, Marshall Cavendish, 2011)

Contents

Introduction   6

1   A Tasty Little Juice Company   9

2   Be Natural   27

3   Be Entrepreneurial   47

4   Be Generous   83

5   Be Commercial   110

6   Be Responsible   140

7   The Future's Fruit   165

Afterword   176

About the Author   191

Introduction

Few brands have risen further and faster towards near-universal affection than Innocent. They had the advantage of a product, using fruit and nothing but fruit, that was recognised as healthy. They had a brand, and a way of communicating with consumers, that brought smiles to people's faces. They caught the mood of the times. They were the little guys winning against the big guys. And they were innocent.

Of course, you expect a 'but'. We all have a cynical streak and Innocent sounded just a little bit too good to be true. The word 'innocent' conjures up images of Adam and Eve in the Garden of Eden, living off fruit, of course. But at some point we all expected Satan to make his entry into this idyll.

The first intimation of this came with Innocent's decision to make its products available on trial in McDonald's. In the previous edition of this book I'd written about the storm that followed that decision. But Innocent had weathered the storm.

The McDonald's trial was defended by Innocent's co-founder Richard Reed on the grounds that it was more responsible to take the opportunity to sell healthy drinks in a family restaurant slated for providing only unhealthy food and drink. Another of Innocent's customers might have said 'Every little helps'. Innocent emerged intact from the situation, possibly even enhanced by the furore – it seemed like a coming of age. Yet there lingered a feeling of regret, expressed by the phrase 'loss of innocence'.

This was a preparation in many ways for the next big storm – the sale of Innocent to Coca-Cola. This was done in stages, first an 18% stake, now a 58% stake. A 58% shareholding implies almost total control of a business. Yet the Innocent founders seemed to have worked out a deal with the new owners that leaves control of all vital business issues in their hands.

How did this happen? When updating this edition, that was the main question to ask. What is the reality of the situation?

Although hindsight is a wonderful thing, I decided with my publishers that the best way to update this edition was to add an Afterword. The Afterword would be able to deal with the ownership issue, and other recent developments that have changed Innocent. We decided against revising the text throughout, with the benefits of hindsight or even the temptations of revisionism. We decided this not from expediency but because this will still give the clearest view of Innocent at this time. To understand Innocent – and to understand it from the viewpoint of those buying it – it helps to see the brand in its fully Innocent days. What did Coke think they were buying? It's easier to understand that by understanding what Innocent was like in the run-up to the change of ownership.

This approach is also, we believe, of greatest value to people in the business world who are thinking about these issues, perhaps hoping or planning to be in a similar situation. How do you make the transition from heroic David to sitting at the right hand of Goliath? It's a common issue for entrepreneurial businesses and there are lessons to be drawn from this story. But, of course, we will all draw different lessons, and the one certain thing is that there is not a single right answer.

Chapter One

A Tasty Little Juice Company

Can we patent what we've done? No, it's just fruit. But now we have a lot of people who have built a lot of knowledge about every aspect of this business. If you do each bit a little better, you end up with a hell of a lot better.

Jon Wright

It's a Monday morning in early April. Outside the sun is shining but winter this year is refusing to shed its overcoat. I walk up to the door of the low industrial building just off the Goldhawk Road in West London. There seems to be a choice of entrances: a window marked "Burglars" and a door marked "People". The cow vans—white with black patches, udders for exhaust and eyelashes over the headlights—wait as a herd outside the store area. Grassy vans, covered in Astroturf with plastic flowers tucked in, line up alongside.

This is Fruit Towers. This is Innocent Drinks. And clearly this is not a conventional British manufacturing company.

I enter and sign in at reception, where I'm offered a smoothie. This is not my first visit so I'm getting used to the routine. Even so, it's always pleasant to pick and choose between a dozen or more different kinds of healthy, delicious drinks. Asking for a coffee would probably lead to a scratching of heads.

All around are the usual paraphernalia of modern office life. Desks, computers, telephones, swivel chairs. A glass-sided meeting room so you can see who is there. Then there is a room with lots of books lying around. And, just by reception, a wall covered with letters, drawings, postcards. This, I am told, is the wall of acclaim. If you read it you'll find that Emily really loves Innocent smoothies. As does Chloe aged 6, especially the mango and passion fruit kind, and Jason, the scout troop, the university friends ... and just about everyone else, it seems.

What is really different is that this space, entered by a domestic-sized door, has Tardis-like qualities. The ceiling is high for what looks like a single-storey building from the outside. As you walk through, there

are working spaces on a level above the ground floor —two floors have been fitted into the space for one. There is an unmistakable sense of energy, people are moving about, not cocooned in their own personal areas or electronic systems. There's a hubbub of voices, but hardly any sound of feet padding about. That's probably because of Fruit Towers' other distinctive feature, the grass underfoot and on the walls.

Of course, it's not real grass but Astroturf. It shines vividly green but it's surprisingly like a carpet to walk on. Or to sit on—which is what most people seem to be doing, because the movement of people has been towards the gathering area in the centre of the building. Here, some 50 or 60 are sitting, lounging or sometimes standing as the regular Monday morning company meeting gets under way.

11

I stand at the back, struggling to catch everything that is being said. But some people project their voices more strongly than others. This is Adam, one of the founders, invited to report on "Europe": "Last week Matt was ill, the Dutch offices were broken into not just once but twice, and on Thursday night the French team got wasted. So this week we'll be concentrating on three things: health, security and sobriety." Someone deeply enfolded in a bean bag calls out the names for the next reports. There are contributions by telephone from Dublin, Paris and Amsterdam. The talk is of sales, facts and figures, stories from each department, reporting on the past week and on what the coming one holds. "We had a meeting with Gala Bingo, fabulous brand, I think you'll agree. And another one at Wimbledon, yes, tennis, that's more like it." The preoccupations of the company emerge in this round-the-room panoramic view of Innocent's business. Showing an advertising campaign. Being listed with a local education authority so that Innocent drinks can go into schools and help children keep healthy. New retail accounts signed up. Testing for antioxidants in new juices. Weekly sales figures. News about competitors. Developing the product strategy. Accountancy qualifications gained and internal scholarships won. Prizes awarded. Spreading the good news of the company's reputation. Here's a report from the driver of one of the vans: "I was in the grassy van last week, dropping off an order. When I got back to the van there was a note on the windscreen—'How are things at Fruit Towers? Wonderful smoothies. Keep it up!'" A round of applause follows. Then everyone is led through a communal stretching exercise.

You might think this sounds impossibly happy-clappy. Your response probably depends on the amount of cynicism you've absorbed into your bloodstream in your life so far. But there is no doubting the relaxed atmosphere, the fact that everyone seems at ease even when having to speak in front of a large audience. And there seems to be no denying that people are enjoying being here and being part of this—and "this" is work.

* * *

Monday morning meeting.

Two years later, revisiting Innocent to update this book, so much has changed yet everything seems much the same. As you go through the front door, a domestic-sized door, it feels even more like stepping inside the Tardis. Innocent has grown in the last two years and it now occupies all the units on this side of the industrial estate. That means they have about twice the space they had two years earlier.

But the atmosphere is the same. They still have Monday morning meetings. It's just that now, with the space opened up and microphones provided, it's much easier to see and hear everyone speak.

13

I'd first come across Innocent in 2001, two years after they'd set up the business. I claim no credit for the discovery because it was a participant on one of my writing workshops who had first pointed them out to me. At the time, I was "writer-in-residence" at Lever Fabergé, part of Unilever. This rather grand title involved running writing workshops for Lever Fabergé's brand and marketing team. I asked the participants on one of those workshops to bring along an example of brand communications that appealed to them, perhaps made them smile. It turned out that Innocent not only made us smile, but also made us laugh. I wrote about this first encounter in my book about brand language *The Invisible Grail*, telling the story of Simon White bringing along three bottles of smoothies and one thickie (yogurt drink).

"Innocent arouse that kind of messianic enthusiasm in people. Simon could have brought a single bottle but he wanted to show the range and variety of the products and the words that they used. "Listen," he said, reading the label of the cranberries and raspberries smoothie.

My mum's started buying our smoothies
(and that's after a whole year, the skinflint).

I've got to behave and not say anything too rude or controversial. So, mum, they are really good for you. They are made with 100% pure fresh fruit. They contain loads of vitamin C (a day and a half's worth). They are as fat free as an apple or banana, and that's because they are just fruit. Is that good enough for you, mum?

Right, I'm off to smash some windows and have a fag.

Everyone enjoyed Simon reading that label out loud, so we got him to read two more. They were just as funny, while still making the serious point that these smoothies are made of fruit and nothing but fruit and they're good for your health. Somehow I believed these words more than a straightforward statement with the same message. Or was it simply that I really took in the message because I had been fully engaged by it?".

* * *

A prototype label from the pre-Innocent days.

My journey had begun, into the Innocent world. Once I had come across them for the first time, they seemed to pop up everywhere—which, given the youth and independence of the company, was remarkable. They seemed to be making all the noise and taking up all the space that you would expect from a big brand coming out of one of the big food companies. But, as they blithely stated, Innocent was about "little tasty drinks".

What were these drinks? The UK consumer was not that familiar with the idea of "smoothies". American consumers were much more steeped in the ways of smoothies, but on this side of the Atlantic the subject needed a little explanation. "What is an Innocent smoothie?" was a question that needed to be answered, and Innocent answered it in their own way: "Well, since you ask, it's a blend of crushed fruit, pure and fresh juices, and absolutely nothing else at all". Or, as recent advertising puts it: "Nothing but nothing but fruit". Or as they put it on one of their early labels:

Thou shalt not commit adultery.

You said it big guy. That's one guideline we follow religiously; our smoothies are 100% pure fruit. We call them innocent because we refuse to adulterate them in any way. Wherever you see the dude (innocent logo) you have got our cross-your-heart-hope-to-die promise that the drink will be completely pure, natural and delicious. If it isn't, you can ring us on the banana phone and make us beg for forgiveness.

Amen.

The simple message from Innocent is that fruit is healthy and additives are not. Any mucking about with the

Poster, 2006 advertising.

ingredients is unnecessary. Fruit contains natural sugar: why add more? Why ship in concentrates made at the fruit picking source (probably overseas) when you could squeeze fresh fruit here and bottle it immediately to preserve that freshness? Why use artificial stabilisers to give a longer shelf life? Why add colourings to ensure a consistent look to inconsistent fruit?

The answers were obvious to existing manufacturers of fruit drinks. They had established these practices because they helped to lower the risks of retailer and consumer rejection, allowed a company's buyers to shop around in the fruit markets, made manufacturing, distribution and logistics easier, and (most of all) reduced costs. From the manufacturers' point of view these are all reasons that hardly need a second thought. They are in a competitive business and they need to get all those things right if they are to prosper by giving consumers what they really want—cheap drinks that taste fruity.

Innocent decided that the answers to those questions were not necessarily quite as cut-and-dried as had been assumed. What if you wanted to arrive at different answers? If Innocent could be really committed to fruit and nothing but fruit, what would be the implications? A more difficult manufacturing process, trickier operations to maintain freshness and quick stock turnover, more rigorous buying policies to source fruit from farms committed to high standards, and a task of persuading consumers of the natural virtues of pure fruit. Plus one other big implication: a higher price to the consumer.

The name Innocent is well chosen, particularly because the founders asked innocent questions and would not be fobbed off with conventional answers. There was a naivety about their innocence that could have been irritating (and no doubt was irritating to

innocent
little tasty drinks

many they questioned). Simply by making smoothies in their own homes they believed that the operational challenges could be met at a larger scale, given the will. In the end, such naivety is not irritating because their instincts were proved right. They trusted that they could find the right people, methods and places to guarantee healthy, tasty drinks. But two challenges remained, two implications needed to be faced. First, the need to charge a premium price; second, the need to persuade consumers of the health benefits that came with a premium product. The answers, though, were not that difficult for three young men with an entrepreneurial, marketing flair. A brand was the answer.

It was the answer, first and foremost, because it was what the founders knew best. There will be more about Adam, Jon and Richard in the next chapter but, for now, these were young, intelligent, Cambridge-educated aspiring entrepreneurs with backgrounds in management consultancy and marketing. They understood brands because that was a large part of their meagre work experience. And they understood brands because they were of that generation, born in the 1970s, who had grown up thinking that business meant providing a service rather than making a widget.

There is a big difference between our understanding of a brand today and our understanding 30 years ago. Brands now are much more the everyday currency of our lives. Rather than thinking that brands are found only on supermarket shelves with names like Omo, Bovril and Hovis—marketing constructs of FMCG (fast moving consumer goods) companies—we are now prepared to see more or less anything as having the potential to be a brand.

In the Great Brand Stories series we have looked at brands called USA, David Beckham, Scotch Whisky and Arsenal. In other times, we would have labelled them a country, a sportsman, a drinks category and a football club. Today, we call them brands because we can define them as having recognisable characteristics that they shape and manage in a relatively consistent way. Brands have personalities that make them like people. People have personalities that make them like brands.

This "cult of personality" certainly began to affect the way we think about brands in the 1990s. The business terminology in the 1980s had been about identity (see, for example, Wally Olins' influential book *The Corporate Personality*, setting out the case for corporate identity).

"Brand" ousted "identity" in the 1990s, partly as a way to make clear that what was being described was more than simply a logo, a visual identifier. This had been an issue for identity consultants in the 1980s too, but, on the whole, they were happy to charge rather large fees for "visual identity". A logo was at the heart of the visual identity system, and it was surrounded by other elements that you could see: colours, photographs or illustrations, typefaces, symbols.

There was some dissatisfaction with this, and the dissatisfaction grew as it seemed harder to claim radical cultural change in companies as a result of a new logo. There is no question that a well-managed company needs a visual identity to project its state of good management. But surely there had to be more than this. How, for example, did companies or brands communicate if they didn't use words? And if you neglect the words you use and the signals sent by your words, what impressions do people have of your brand—whatever the beauty might be of your logo?

This is all rather a crash course in design/identity/ brand developments in the last two decades of the 20th century. But this book is not the place for the full history so I hope readers will accept the thrust of the argument (perhaps reinforced by my assertion that "I was there at the time"). This rapid explanation is necessary, however, to provide some context to explain why Innocent, in 1999, seemed such a breath of fresh air—particularly to people in the business world with interest in branding and marketing.

The situation was that more and more was being claimed for brands (much of it with some justification) and more and more complex branding models were being devised. Brand consultancies used the models to

Poster, 2003 Advertising.

justify fees that seemed impossible to justify if the outcome really was simply a new logo. However, much as they talked about brand values, personality and characteristics as if they were analysing human beings rather than corporations, the brands that emerged seemed devoid of humour and humanity. A large part of that was down to the words. As the focus of attention was shifted away from the visual, there was a realisation that actually words were rather important. Perhaps a brand's "tone of voice"—or even its "verbal identity" —could not only help differentiate it from competitors but also create bonds of affection and loyalty with different audiences.

Innocent were not the first to realise this, or the first to demonstrate it. But suddenly, with the new millennium, they seemed to provide proof that words worked. Words could be the most important element in creating a brand. It so happened that there were many people— commentators, writers, brand consultants, me—who were looking at this question with expectation and hope of evidence. Could engaging words be the basis for a successful brand? Innocent arrived and "yes" seemed to be the answer.

The Innocent founders understood this intuitively but they would not have gone through an analytical process to lead them to such a conclusion. I suspect that lack of money to spend on visual identity was a greater influence on their word-biased approach. And the fact that they were all rather good with words. Their instincts were that words were good for getting on with people, for establishing relationships, for making people smile and warm towards you, for winning people to your side, for persuading others to trust you and (perhaps) to give you money. Now, what does a brand have to do ...?

23

That is one aspect of the times that was absolutely perfect for Innocent. The wave was rolling and they rode on top of it. But they happened to find a second wave. This was something that they were completely conscious of, indeed it was the foundation of the business. Innocent Drinks was set up as a healthy company making a healthy product in increasingly health-conscious times.

Richard Reed tells a story, which he insists is true, of parents gathering to collect their children from school. One mother sees her child in the playground eating an apple and screams out: "Take that fuckin' apple out of your mouth, you won't have room for your chips". Innocent was set up by the three founders because they were all conscious of their relatively unhealthy lifestyles and of the need to eat and drink more healthily. As well as enabling themselves to consume more healthy produce, they were keen to avoid adding to the unhealthy eating problem with yet more additives. They always wanted, and always stated, that Innocent would be "a business we can be proud of". So they had to start with the product itself, and what could be healthier than unadulterated fruit? Even if that meant that the product would be relatively expensive. Richard expressed it like this: "Bad food is bad value. You're not doing me a favour if you give me bad food 10p cheaper. It's worth spending those few extra pence. The more natural stuff you get inside you, the longer you'll live."

In 1999, when Innocent launched, we were just getting familiar with the idea of five portions of fruit and vegetables a day to keep healthy. Reports were coming from all directions about the rise in obesity, links between bad nutrition and bad health and behaviour, the role of food manufacturers in creating or adding to the problem through the over-processing of food, the use of chemical additives, the excess of sugar, salt and fat in our diets. At the same time, there was a rising awareness among many people that other options were worth pursuing. More people were joining gyms and working out as part of their lifestyles, organic food was becoming more sought-after and widely available, people started checking E numbers on ingredients lists and choosing healthier options. This trend accelerated in the following years. Films like *Supersize Me* drew attention to the potential unhealthiness of a McDonald's diet. Chefs and cooking programmes became all the rage on TV, and one of those chefs, Jamie Oliver, started a campaign based on his reality TV show to improve the quality of school dinners. The choice between good and bad food became an emotive issue, surrounded by moral arguments directed at the big manufacturing companies. Guilty of poisoning us with chemicals, was the charge. And a little juice company in West London seemed to make its position clear through its name, Innocent.

Innocent set out to make healthy fruit drinks and they have stuck to that. They have not wavered from their mission to be healthy, they have not compromised by allowing any synthetic ingredients into their drinks. This remains an important point of difference when in 2006 it was reported that a fast food chain version of a strawberry milk shake contained 59 artificial ingredients just to make the flavouring. Those ingredients are on top of sugar, stabilisers and other additives that have nothing to do with imparting "flavour".

So, Innocent make drinks that taste good and do you good. They promise never to use concentrates, stabilisers, flavouring, GM stuff, preservatives, added sugar, E numbers. And if they do you can tell their mums. That sets the disarming tone and helps to explain how, in less than ten years, they have crept up on us to become the fastest growing company in the UK's food and drink industry. It's the brand that did it. A large part of Innocent's success has to be put down to its brand because, unlike many other companies, it offers few other suspects. There is no vast product range, there is no big financial backing from a multinational, there is no technological breakthrough hitting the market at just the right time. It's simply the product—fruit and nothing but fruit drinks. And the brand—Innocent. Of course, the drinks are tasty *and* healthy, and they did happen along at a time when many people started to feel that a little help towards a healthier lifestyle might be useful. The three young men who founded Innocent were also representatives of the market for Innocent. There's a deceptively laid-back streak of idealism—even if we can't save the world, we don't want to destroy it. But we still want to enjoy life, have a laugh with friends, and reserve the right to get drunk occasionally. And when that happens, a pure fruit drink is the kind of hangover cure that convinces you that it must be doing you good.

They convinced enough of us to give it a try—and to keep on going back for more. The main weapon they used was humour. We laughed with them, we liked them and wanted them to succeed. We bought into the idea of the Innocent brand, a brand built around five principles: be natural, be entrepreneurial, be generous, be commercial, be responsible. Those principles also provide the structure for the five chapters that follow.

Chapter Two

Be Natural

So far, in our own small way, we've shown you can be successful and ethical. We make food that's good for people—most branded food companies can't say that.

Richard Reed

Cambridge has built a reputation for innovation and intellect. It's an academic place where people have studied for centuries: mathematics, philosophy, literary theory, quantum physics. Its roll call of famous people includes Sir Isaac Newton, Charles Darwin, Crick and Watson, F R Leavis and half of Monty Python. It also includes Adam Balon, Richard Reed and Jon Wright, the three founders of Innocent Drinks.

Cambridge is important to the Innocent story because the three would probably not have met otherwise. But they did meet at the same college, St John's, and they became friends. The friendship continued beyond Cambridge. University friendships can be the most enduring but they seldom extend to setting up in business together. And, for the first couple of years after Cambridge, they each went their separate ways into working life.

Jon Wright was an engineer, and he joined the management consultancy Bain & Co. For three years, he did project-based work, with different companies, industries and countries.

Adam Balon joined McKinsey as a consultant, then went to Virgin where he was in marketing. He was one of the Virgin Cola team, taking on Pepsi and Coke.

Richard Reed went into advertising, on the account management side (as he discloses with a smile), working for the leading agency BMP.

These were the conventional career paths of high-flying Cambridge graduates. No doubt the university patted itself on the back. Jon, Adam and Richard were reasonably pleased with themselves, seeming set on interesting and lucrative careers. And, because this is important to Innocent, their mums were probably happy too. Three years passed; Jon, Adam and Richard stayed

Jon Wright.

Adam Balon.

Richard Reed.

in touch and met regularly. When they met, whether for a social drink or a holiday away together, they talked about what they were doing. How's your interesting job? It's interesting but...There was always the feeling that there should be more, not so much to make more money but to feel more fulfilled. They kept talking about the possibility of setting up a business together.

Jon Wright explains: "We were driving down a French motorway at two in the morning, going on a skiing holiday. We were talking to keep ourselves awake. We'd talked about it before but this time we decided we had to come up with something. We had to get serious. The idea emerged, second or third idea in. We could make smoothies. We agreed we would have a proper meeting after the holiday."

It seemed that the idea for smoothies emerged because they felt a little guilty about their own health. They were all working hard and finding too little time for fitness and diet. Their daily token bow to healthiness was a fruit juice, "the one bit of health in the day". They also knew how to make fruit juice as they had juicers at home. They decided that if they were going to take a big leap into the unknown and start up a business, they would be best sticking to something simple that they could make themselves. Not that there was any thought of a lifetime to be spent cutting fruit at the kitchen table. But if the manufacturing could be relatively easy then they would have more of their own intellectual resources to devote to marketing and selling—and building a brand.

Jon continues the story. "At Bain, I'd been amazed that there were always similarities, from the point of view of a manufacturing engineer, between different processes and products. You always seemed to approach problems in a common way. Here there was no new technology to develop. If we knew how to make it, then we also knew how to sell it—because effectively we would be selling it to ourselves, to people like us who were buying juices for that daily dose of health."

"So we sat there and asked ourselves: 'Who's going to do what?' Adam said: 'I fancy commercial and sales'. Richard was marketing. My role was operations. There was no dispute, it all fell into place."

The only area of possible dispute was the marketing role. In many ways, with his Virgin Cola background Adam had more hands-on, relevant experience than Richard. Richard had been an advertising man and did not yet have the full range of marketing expertise. But Adam fancied sales and that was that. The three slotted neatly into three roles but each agreed that they would have a perfect right to question and challenge the others—because the reality was, no-one was an expert. Richard stresses, though: "We came in at 'keep everything natural'. That was the idea, a simple thought that informs everything."

Then the hard work began. From March 1998, they put in three months of intensive work at evenings and weekends, fitting in the development of the business around their day jobs. It involved a lot of research into how to make smoothies as well as into the market and business context. It was an exhausting time and at the end of it Jon confessed what he had been doing to his mentor at Bain. The mentor, Glen, advised him to take three months' leave of absence.

There was now a target in mind. For the previous two years, Adam and Richard had organised a little music festival at Parsons Green in West London. It was a low-key, local event, and in previous years they had done it for fun. Now they decided to do it for their final piece of research. The Innocent story is littered with pieces of "luck", as they cheerfully admit. The luck at this stage was to find someone who could make smoothies for them in sufficient quantities to sell at the Jazz on the Green festival in September.

"We'd made the drinks," Richard explains. "We had the recipes and we'd tried them out with friends and family. But we'd made them in our own kitchens. We needed someone and luckily enough we found a crazy carrot farmer called Geoff in Nottinghamshire. He grew his own carrots and squeezed them in his own carrot press, at the side of his carrot field. Geoff was fixated by his tractor, it was the way of getting fast from field to bottle, keeping everything fresh. Our first brand name was Fast Tractor. Anyway, Geoff had a tractor but also a fruit press and a bottling line. We met him in Adam's offices and agreed a deal. We didn't have much money but we decided to spend it on fruit that Geoff would crush and bottle, and that we would sell at Jazz on the Green. We drove the bottled smoothies down from Nottinghamshire in a van."

Jazz on the Green, artist's impression.

The Innocent founding story is now famous. It is also true. You don't necessarily need truth to create a myth or legend, but the truth has served Innocent well. Here is the founding story, as it first appeared on their website.

> "In the summer of 1998 when we had developed our first smoothie recipes but were still nervous about giving up our proper jobs, we bought £500 worth of fruit, turned it into smoothies and sold them from a stall at a little music festival in London. We put up a big sign saying 'Do you think we should give up our jobs to make these smoothies?' and put out a bin saying 'YES' and a bin saying 'NO' and asked people to put the empty bottle in the right bin. At the end of the weekend the 'YES' bin was full so we went in the next day and resigned."

That's simple, effective storytelling. It set the tone for Innocent. Behind the natural but now practised insouciance was a great deal of anxiety, as Jon admits: "It had been the hottest weekend of the year. Everything had gone well for us. But that evening it sank in. We didn't really decide, the decision was made for us. But that festival had been like throwing a party in your own house, a one-off. Now we had to keep doing it."

So, with a deep gulp, they were off and running. The next nine months, until the official launch in May 1999, was probably the toughest period in Innocent's short history. "The hardest time was early," says Adam. "Waiting for things to happen, waiting for wholesalers.

Waiting...frustrating. It was important that we kept each other's heads up. We knew it would be stressful but we kept telling ourselves 'we'll get through it'."

Money was an issue, as with any business. Finance had been the parcel that kept getting passed around. No-one had a yearning towards accountancy, whereas the three roles of operations, sales and marketing had fallen naturally into place. They had all thought that funding should be straightforward because they were now very clear about the proposition. They approached banks, who turned them down. They tried venture capitalists, who turned them down in more brutal ways. "OK, so you're up against Coke and you know nothing." Imagine a reality TV programme where they had to go into the dragon's den and make a case for investment— only to receive hollow laughs and solid sneers. This was the time of dotcoms, the time when it seemed that ready money was available for anything technological. There is very little technology in fruit. Ten presentations came and went, and they were getting nowhere. So, in desperation or bravado, they sent out an email to all the the friends and contacts they could think of. The gist of the message was straightforward: "Does anybody know anybody rich?"

A guardian angel emerged from the ether. Maurice Pinto has become a figure of some reverence in Innocent folklore. And, of course, he is an angel, one of the small breed of wealthy people who are described as business angels. Cap in one hand, notebook in the other, I went to see him.

* * *

I have an appointment to see Maurice Pinto in Mayfair. "I don't think he's in yet, sir, but go up to the first floor." The lift stands there unused and mistrusted, as if last time it had detained visitors embarrassingly between floors. The first floor reception is small, with three lady receptionists who are of that shrinking breed of lady receptionists, now on the brink of retirement or perhaps extinction. Leading from reception are corridors with rooms that are now offices but might once have been living rooms. If you strip out the computers, these rooms would have looked much the same 100 years ago. If this had been my first encounter with Innocent, I would have been completely thrown. But, of course, this is not Innocent. This is Maurice Pinto.

Here is the man himself, apologising for slight lateness. It really is no problem at all, I've enjoyed the opportunity to take in these surroundings. But there are a couple of unexpected things about Maurice Pinto, apparent on first sight and first hearing. He is well past retirement age and there is the twang of a refined American accent.

I follow him to his office, and he sits down at an antique desk. First, he checks his emails on the computer. Maurice sits there in pinstripe suit, crisp shirt, sober tie and braces. He has a kindly face that has experienced the full gamut of business emotions, the ups and downs of making and losing money. But, from his readiness to ease into a smile, the impression is that he has seen more ups than downs. Every so often, for gently theatrical effect, he uses his rimless glasses to help the conversation along, taking them off, polishing them, putting them back on.

I am interested to hear the Innocent story from his viewpoint. Most people in Innocent are aged about

30, but Maurice is quick to inform me that he is 72. Yet there really is no reason to suppose that age has done anything to blunt his sharpness. How had he found Jon, Adam and Richard when he first met them?

"They wanted to start a company with the idea of creating a brand. That was very clear. Smoothies were simply the vehicle.

And everything they've done since has stayed true to that. They've doggedly stuck to doing nothing that would diminish the brand. No own label, for example. That's my abiding recollection, they were totally focused on the brand. That and the fact they were obviously nice boys. Middle-class boys. Jon from Guildford, Adam from London, Richard from Yorkshire. Nothing of the barrow boy about them—not the Philip Greens of this world."

Early days.

The "boys" had told me that first discussions with Maurice had soon veered away from the details of the business plan. They had talked about life and what they were like as people, rather than the nuts and bolts of finance and management. Maurice's model is to find people not businesses. This was quickly apparent from the way he talked but, when needed, there was a sharp focus back on business detail.

"I first heard about them through a colleague of Jon's at Bain, David Whittaker. We shared an office, and he wanted me to see them. I turned that down at first, but David insisted hard, and I agreed to read the business plan. It struck me that it was extremely well written, and I read the whole thing. It was a sophisticated plan. The premise was that the US market demonstrated that there was a serious market for smoothies. The argument was that that was transferable to the UK. In the UK, there was only PJ's, but the belief was that the product was not really up to snuff. However, they had established a useful beach-head so we could piggyback on that by attacking with a better product.

"This was interesting, so I agreed to meet them. They turned up looking unconventional. Most people in these situations at least put on a tie. They were as scruffy as hell but good-looking boys, clearly bright and very articulate. They were fun to be with. One bizarre aspect was just the question, 'Who's in charge?' They insisted all three were, it was collegiate, there was no first among equals. As you know, that violates Chapter Three of the Venture Capital Handbook."

There is a twinkle in his eye as he whips off his glasses. He goes on to describe several meetings when they got to know each other and came up with an accepted structure for the financing. Maurice introduced the business to partners who invested together—angels not institutions. Everyone had a bit of scepticism: "What

Really lovely juices.

do they really know about juice?" But Maurice stuck to it. To him in 1999 a quarter of a million pounds did not seem a lot; he had recently made a good return from a big deal. He agreed to put up the money for a 20 per cent stake, intending to share the risk with his investing partners. However, one by one the partners turned him down. So here was an irritating quandary.

"No-one else came in, but I felt I'd given a commitment. The options were to tell them 'No' even though I'd said 'Yes', or to fund it entirely myself. I felt committed, there was a capital gains tax advantage that year—and I thought they had an outside chance of succeeding. Perhaps there was just a five per cent chance of it becoming a good business. With any investment I reckon there's a 50 per cent chance of non-failure but only a ten per cent chance of real success. This was a risk. How can a little company succeed in the juice business?"

Maurice took certain steps to increase the chances of "non-failure". He brought in Jules Hydleman as chairman because he had merchanting experience. He established meetings every two months.

"They were always professional. They came with their charts and slides, and we discussed strategic issues. As time went on I was surprised that they never came back and asked for more money. There was no need."

For seven years Maurice Pinto has been Innocent's sole investor. This puts him in a unique position. He backed his judgement of three people and a business plan with a quarter of a million pounds of his own money. Now he talks about introducing his son (an investment banker) to Innocent the next time he's over from New York. Innocent is not a family business but it has pulled off that difficult trick for a business of creating a sense of family. As with any family, there are exasperations.

"What drives me crazy at times is the slow decision-making. I thought young people would make decisions quickly but they worry decisions to death; it goes on and on. But, looking back, I can say I've never worked with a management team that has a higher hit rate with its decisions. It's the best management team I've ever

worked with. Their intellectual content is high—and they
hire more people like that. I recently ran a workshop for
them, with a lot of new people, and they all had Firsts.
Intellect has a lot to do with their success—that and
huge motivation. But they are seriously *tough*, in the best
sense, in the way they look at people and themselves."

There is more from Maurice, but this completes his story
of the early days. We carried on talking about the way
the business has progressed, and he takes something
of a paternal pride in it all. It probably could not
have happened without him but perhaps his greatest
achievement has been knowing not to interfere too
much. He recognised the quality of the people, backed
his judgement, but then stepped back until further advice
was needed. The name "angel" seems appropriate for
once.

And in 2008, Maurice still has his wings neatly
folded and he smiles beatifically on from the sidelines.
He retains his investment, having adopted the wise
strategy of not selling for as long as the founders aren't
selling.

* * *

From the end of the Jazz on the Green festival to the launch in May 1999 was a rocky period. Tensions were high, finance was uncertain for much of the time, and Richard, Jon and Adam had given up well-paid jobs. They went out meeting as many people as they could. They would often go off to meetings singly, rather than as a group of three, because that enabled them to see more people. Many times, two of them would return dispirited, saying "this isn't going to work", but the third had had a different experience. They pulled each other through.

This was an important toughening experience. It meant that they really challenged the idea before they formally set up the business, making sure it was robust and not half-baked. By the time Maurice Pinto was ready to pledge his money, they decided to say to him: "Don't give us the money until the product tastes great, until we have a name we like and until we know we can make some money." Embedded in there was a personal commitment from each founder, saying in effect we guarantee to get operations, marketing and sales right.

They always had a clear idea of what they wanted to be. They wrote down the words at an early stage: to make fresh, healthy, natural drinks, to be Europe's favourite little juice company. As Maurice Pinto discovered, with a sense of admiring irritation, they did not rush into decisions. It was a game of thinking ahead, anticipating where they would be in 12 months' time so that they could get ahead of the supply chain. They drew on the experience gained at Bain, McKinsey, Virgin and BMP to get everything lined up—and to make sure that good relationships were established with suppliers.

They needed all their charm to achieve that. Having decided that they wanted everything to be natural, they pursued this objective like zealots, with a mixture of naivety and bloody-mindedness. They wanted to make smoothies like you make them at home, but in much larger quantities. They went to suppliers and asked questions. The suppliers all said they should use concentrate, stabilisers or add sugar. But they kept asking, "Why?" And to every negative answer they asked "Why?" again until eventually the suppliers agreed that what they were asking for was possible. They chipped away at the objections until they got their own way.

Importantly, they made commitments. At the beginning they agreed to take most of the risk, to make reparations at their own cost if things went wrong. They were taking people on a journey and people went along, staying on board because it kept working. The same team that printed labels originally is still printing the labels but now in millions rather than hundreds. The same questioning, challenging approach with suppliers continues. "Why not this way?" is the question constantly asked. Not much has changed except scale, and the fact that it's no longer the founders who set their alarms to go off at three so they can drive around London delivering smoothies.

Innocent smoothies. Innocent Drinks. The name came and the brand that it represents, giving confidence that the second of the three promises to Maurice would be fulfilled. After a brief flirtation with Fast Tractor, the name Innocent (usually written with a lower case 'i' on brand communications) was chosen. It expressed everything they wanted the brand to be. A brand *without* the guilt of adding unnatural ingredients. But *with* a tone of cheeky mates who are playing at being simpler

Delivery boys.

than they are. And doing no harm to the environment, employees, customers or anyone else they come into contact with. It was a lot to live up to but as soon as the first bottles appeared with labels on, it was unmistakably right.

Of course, they tested the brand concept but not with masses of market research. They asked friends and family, people they trusted, and the answers gave them confidence to go ahead and try to sell. This was Adam's area but, as he explains, everyone was (and still is) involved in the selling process.

43

"Our first sale was to a little café called 'Out to Lunch'. It was almost next to where we had our office. We were working in Ladbroke Grove. There were lots of studios with interesting businesses and this was the café on the corner. So Jon just went in there and came out with the sale—£24. We were desperate to know if the smoothies had sold to customers, so we went back at the end of the day but the café was shut. So we tried to peek in through the window. It had high windows so we stood on milk crates. We could just see the fridge, just make out that half the bottles were gone. That's still our best sale. In the early days, we had to work for every bottle sold, touring Fitzrovia, Ladbroke Grove, places we thought were likely, just knocking on doors."

Their first conversations with Maurice Pinto had included talk about other products. But smoothies were always the first choice because "be natural" was the principle that drove them. When thinking about brand names the question asked was, "Is it cool?" They visualised names applied to, say, a club night or a T-shirt to help answer that question, but not because they ever planned to do such things with the brand. Above all, they agreed that they wanted to create "a business to be proud of".

When I interviewed Richard about the development of the brand, I wondered aloud whether the commitment to "be natural" and maintain Innocent's very laid-back image meant that they did everything by instinct. In particular, did they all just know what the brand stood for? It seemed that way, so I assumed that there was no formal definition of the Innocent brand and its values.

"Oh yes, there is. Because we're geeks. Not right from day one, but early on, we've had a model. There are brand principles. We'd decided that Innocent was going to be this natural, inclusive brand, but of course the drinks had to be brilliant. Given that, we felt we needed principles to focus on. They codify

the brand but we don't use them as a catechism.
We prefer just to meet people and see if they get it.
A brand is what it does, not what it says it is."

The company values are not that radically different from those you might have seen adopted by other brands. The difference is that Innocent takes them rather more seriously. Although Richard stresses that these are not used as a catechism, there is no doubt that people in Innocent are aware of the need to embrace the values. A business is nothing more than a community of human beings. How do you engage with that community? Rita Clifton, the chairman of Interbrand, always talks about the brand needing to be the central organising system of a business. Brands need to use their values—and the way they have defined them—to guide how they go about every aspect of their business: from where they source and make the product to the "terms and conditions" for every employee.

Innocent is an example of this in practice. Yet they are aware of the dangers of seeming to be weird evangelists. It's a self-awareness that prevents them developing any Moonie-like tendencies. And, because they abide by their values, they avoid falling into the trap of corporate pomposity. *Do it better than anyone else, and have fun doing it.* They stick by that but this principle itself allows a little bit of latitude in the way they assess themselves. So they apply different, but very human, tests to their own behaviour. For example, when appointing new staff—to any position in the company there is the Van Test. "Would you be happy to spend an afternoon driving around with this person in the van?"

Perhaps most crucially there is the Nursing Home Test. This was agreed by the founders in the early days of the business. *Only make decisions you can be proud of when you're older.* There is a large element of idealism there, some might say impossible idealism. Rather than impossible, they would call it Innocent.

Innocent Company Values

Be Natural
Keep it human, put people first.
Make 100% natural, delicious, healthy stuff, 100% of the time.
Treat others, especially our drinkers, as we want to be treated.

Be Entrepreneurial
Chase opportunities and be responsive.
Be creative and challenge the status quo.
Do it better than anyone else, and have fun doing it.

Be Responsible
Be true to our principles, and do what we believe is right.
To be conscious of the consequences of our actions in both the short and long term.
To leave things a little better than we find them,
and to encourage others to join us too.

Be Commercial
Create growth and profit for us and our customers.
Be tough, but fair.
Think clearly, act decisively and keep the main thing, the main thing.

Be Generous
When offering praise to others.
With our time when coaching others.
With rewards when people deliver.
With charitable support.

Chapter Three

Be Entrepreneurial

Always think little. Take care of the details. Once you're a big company you forget about the details.

Dan Germain

Dan Germain.

It might surprise him a little to be an exemplar of entrepreneurialism but Dan Germain is the central character of this chapter. When you meet people from Innocent to talk about their time in the company, most of them describe themselves with a number. Dan is Number 4. That simply means that Dan was the fourth person to join Innocent, way back in the very early days. The three founders were there and Dan will immediately tell you that they are the entrepreneurs. He should know, because he has known them (inevitably, it seems) from being at Cambridge with them. And, given a little prompting, he could tell some stories about the events they used to run (to make money) at Cambridge ...

Dan Germain is someone who would pass the Van Test with just about anyone you can think of: your mum, that irritating next-door neighbour or even Uncle George who insists on playing with his false teeth. And Dan would probably put up with them without once losing his temper. Dan is big and bearded, the archetypal gentle giant, with all the outward appearance of being completely laid-back. He has all the charm and good humour of the founding three, but without the obvious sense of inner drive that emanates from them. But we all know that appearances can be deceptive. He would be an ideal candidate to be best man at a wedding.

Dan is Innocent's "Creative Head". As Number 4 he is also "Guardian Angel", and he used to be "People's Champion". That's enough titles to be giving anyone before confusion starts to set in. Dan is Guardian Angel because he looks after the spirit of the company. Having been there almost from the start, and having known Adam, Richard and Jon since before Innocent, Dan has a feel for the soul of the company, what fits and what doesn't fit. He's probably a bit of a talisman, like the ravens in the tower, his presence a visible sign that Innocent remains true to its principles.

Being Creative Head puts him in a good position to watch over the spirit of Innocent and make sure it does not start saying anything that is other than Innocent. So Dan is responsible for the look, feel and, above all, the words that represent the brand.

Signage, Fruit Towers.

This is not a solitary responsibility, though, as Dan is always first to emphasise. Everyone in Innocent has creative input to make. It starts with the founders. Richard, with responsibility for marketing and coming from an ad agency background, has the most obvious creative credentials—although in that rather weird way of ad agencies he was not counted there as one of the "creatives". It was Richard who wrote the first Innocent words that appeared on labels, who set the style, the tone of voice that has continued ever since. Adam, coming from a marketing job in Virgin, will never be a conventional, numbers-fixated commercial director. And Jon, head of operations and with a solid engineering background, designed the original Innocent labels.

Clearly the company is built on creativity to an unusual degree. Analysed in one way, Innocent is a manufacturing company: it makes fruit drinks. But in reality the creative expression of the Innocent brand has enabled it to succeed in a way that few other manufacturing companies have succeeded in recent times. This is a company that loves creative ideas and encourages them from everyone. Dan's next-in-line, writing stories on labels, was first another Dan who originally joined as an accountant. And now it's Ceri who switched across from marketing.

Innocent is, therefore, a thoroughly modern company. It sees its brand as a prime asset and a creative catalyst, as well as the touchstone that guides everything that happens. The question "Is that Innocent?" will decide every judgement that needs to be made about the direction of the business. It will always be judged against the criteria of the five values. In Dan's case, when assessing the creative output of the company, the injunction to "be entrepreneurial" will be called to mind.

Because that means being creative and challenging the status quo, and then doing it better than anyone else and having fun while doing it. Within those words, what unites the creative and the entrepreneurial thoughts is the constant awareness of others. Innocent is always wanting to be different from and better than anyone else.

Dan's role is crucial, therefore, as interpreter of all things Innocent, and the shaper of Innocent's everyday language. For a company to give the brand such primacy is still unusual. And for a company to give language such a leading role in the projection of the brand is even more unusual.

So it is worth focusing on Innocent's creativity, because this is what makes it distinctively entrepreneurial, and on Dan's role in expressing it. We live in a business world where companies increasingly pay lip service at least to the importance of creativity.

All the great work comes from people's obsession and imagination, not from focus groups.

Sir Michael Grade, ITV and former BBC chairman

Planning by its very nature, defines and preserves categories. Creativity, by its very nature, creates categories or re-arranges established ones.

Professor Henry Mintzberg, management guru

Our only asset is the human imagination.

Microsoft

I had first taken note of Innocent because of their words on labels, whether written by Richard or Dan. Neither

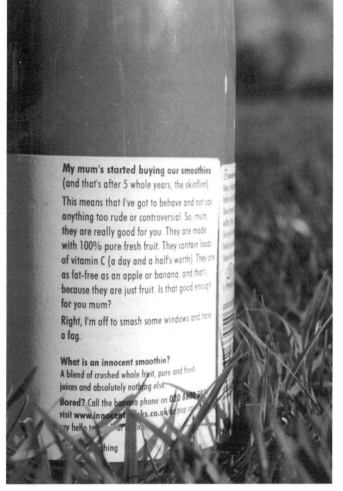

My mum's started buying our smoothies (and that's after 5 whole years, the skinflint).

This means that I've got to behave and not say anything too rude or controversial. So, mum, they are really good for you. They are made with 100% pure fresh fruit. They contain loads of vitamin C (a day and a half's worth). They are as fat-free as an apple or banana, and that's because they are just fruit. Is that good enough for you mum?

Right, I'm off to smash some windows and have a fag.

What is an innocent smoothie?
A blend of crushed whole fruit, pure and fresh juices and absolutely nothing else.

Bored? Call the banana phone on 020 8600 3?? visit www.innocent ks.co.uk or pop r?
ay hello t?
thing

An early label.

will now say who wrote what, perhaps because they have forgotten, perhaps because they prefer the author to be known as Innocent. Much as I enjoyed the smoothies, it was the constantly changing stories on the bottle labels that kept me buying new ones. As well as the stories, many of which you can read in this chapter, there was the fun to be had with every detail of language. Rather than a "sell by" or "use by" date there was an "enjoy by" date. There was play to be had with legal marks. TM would be said to stand for tasty mixture rather than trade mark, and the copyright sign could mean chicken-free. Generally, these variants on the standard legal phrases come out of the stories themselves, so they are not generic but jokes that make a point. TM equalled "three more", for example, when a new and improved smoothie was introduced with extra strawberries ...

Even the ingredients lists were both funny and meaningful. As well as the fruit ingredients listed—12 strawberries, 3 oranges, 50 cranberries and so on—there are some occasional, unexpected additions. Two plump nuns, three traffic cones, a small church, for example. It can take you aback for a second but you quickly realise that the local nunnery has not been harvested, only the fruit farm. And that is the point, the ingredients are fruit, nothing but fruit.

It was startling and refreshing. It probably made you think better of the drink that you had no doubt enjoyed. Those smoothies tasted good, and they also made you laugh. When Dan Germain started, he had the same reaction too. He agreed to help out his mates because it seemed an amusing way to spend some time before going back to university where he intended to do a further degree.

"I had no intention of staying. It was just a stop on
the way back to academic life. So I mucked in and
did a bit of everything, in the stores, the vans,
the office. After a month or so, Richard said, 'Do
you fancy having a go?' and he passed the latest label
brief to me. Somehow I found myself staying. Richard's
a great writer. In an ad agency we could have been a
great creative team. So we've become that outside the ad
agency. He's madly enthusiastic, his energy's infectious
—and I know if it makes him laugh, it's all right. It's
that old thing about writing with one person in mind."

"The other side of it is just thinking if there's someone
who really wouldn't find that the least bit funny. If
your mum disapproves, for example. The message is
the most important thing. It's the same message: the
drinks taste amazing and they're good for you. Now
that would get very boring if you just kept saying it
in the same way, so varying the delivery is vital. It's
like being with your friends, your dialogue changes.
But we try to keep that tone of talking to mates."

There is a part of Dan that is deeply resistant to the
examination of Innocent's language. There is almost a
sense of superstition that if you capture and pin it like a
butterfly on a board, you will have killed it.

"It's always been other people who have pointed
out the words. We just chat with people on the labels.
It's the hardest thing in the world to analyse it. It's
like analysing what I said to my dad on the phone
last night. All it is, is the way Innocent speaks. We've
always written that way. I don't want to cut open the
Golden Goose only to find out we've just killed it."

Dan sees the way Innocent speaks as part of an overall
trend in consumer-facing businesses. Consumers are
more clued up, they will no longer believe whatever the
company thinks they should believe. There needs to be
more of a gentle wooing process, recognising that
people are more likely to make up their own minds or

to take the word of a friend rather than a corporation. People want a sense of the reality that lies behind the image. Perhaps gallingly for Innocent, although they laugh it off lightly, they have become the UK's most imitated brand. Simply because their language is so refreshingly distinctive, it is their verbal style that other brands try to mimic, very rarely with any success.

Here are two examples I came across recently, both brands using a style of words that they would not have contemplated five years ago. The first is from Burger King, on one of their bags:

> The great thing about a take-away bag is finishing your meal. Firstly, because you're left with that gloating look of satisfaction and secondly you usually find a couple of loose, renegade fries. It's like when you put on a pair of trousers and find a fiver in the pocket. It's the simple things ...

That's bad enough as a pale, second-hand imitation but the second example, from Real Chips, is even worse. The front of the crisp packet says:

> REAL. WHAT IS PATATAS BRAVAS FLAVOUR? WELL, APART FROM BEING A DELICIOUS SPANISH DISH, IT IS MORE IMPORTANTLY A LIGHTHOUSE. IT ALERTS THE WORLD TO OUR STANDARDS. ILLUMINATES OUR TRUE SPIRIT. AND WARNS THE EATER 'DELICIOUS AND TASTY HANDCOOKED CHIPS UP AHEAD.'*

The back of pack says:

> *PATATAS BRAVAS IS ALSO A GAUNTLET OR GLOVE THROWN DOWN AT THE FEET OF OUR COMPETITORS, CHALLENGING THEM TO 100% NATURAL INGREDIENTS. TO RAISE THE BAR, TO THINK OUTSIDE THE BAG ... TO ROCK US FROM OUR THRONE. IF THEY DARE.

The capital letters, as they appear on the packet, are appropriate in capturing the unsubtle nature of the communication. Perhaps there are several layers of post-modern irony going on there, but the effect on me is completely alienating. They seem to have attempted the kind of analysis that Dan dreads and come up with only half the right answers—contradicted by the other half that are completely wrong. The clunky use of the asterisk reminds me, not to the advantage of Real Crisps, of my favourite joke on an Innocent label. Advised to shake the bottle to mix up the fruit contents, the wording says "separation can sometimes occur*". Lower down the label the asterisk is picked up, and the message expanded: *"but mummy still loves daddy."

The unfortunate fact is that Innocent's success has spawned a lot of inferior versions of "chatty language" on packaging. There is a not-for-profit association of writers called 26 (www.26.org.uk) which exists to champion the cause of better writing in everyday life and a greater love of words in business. Many of its members are copywriters, working with businesses and creative agencies. Stories started appearing on the members' message board about being given briefings that went along the lines of "Can you write it like Innocent?" Dan, who is also a member of 26, added his contribution to the message board.

> "I always found it a bit odd that people might want to sound a bit like us. It seems to me that the only thing they should ever really want to sound like is themselves. The tone that Innocent uses is the one that we use when we're talking to our mums or messing about in the pub on a Friday night. It didn't get invented or agreed upon after a period of consultancy with some expert toners, and so what you hear from us is us. Not someone else's idea of what we are. Of course, analysing it like this is

the toughest thing of all, because it makes you sound like a bit of an overly analytical nob, and that's the last thing we want to be. Fundamentally, I believe that a company will do best when it has its own natural voice. But that might be the tricky bit—finding out what your voice is when you've been somebody else's for too long."

I asked Will Awdry, one of European advertising's finest writers and creative head of the agency DDB (but since moved to Ogilvy), how he would describe Innocent's tone of voice. "Innocent's great power is its consistency of voice. The accents in the voice are innocence, truth, fun, wholesomeness, wit, spirit, lack of pomposity, honesty and lightness of touch. Not a bad chord of notes for any player." But quite a difficult chord for people to play if they cannot read the music.

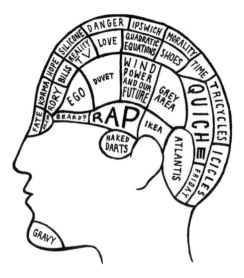

A nice picture from the *Innocent Smoothie Recipe Book*, 4th Estate, 2006.

The relationship between Dan and Richard is one of those easygoing friendships where you wonder if there might be something in telepathy. They understand each other's thinking, which must have made it easy for the writing to pass seamlessly from Richard to Dan. It is the natural Innocent way for people to learn from each other simply by doing the job. In those early days Dan became the People's Champion (a title later passed on to Rowena). Labels have always invited Innocent drinkers to get in touch: drop in at Fruit Towers, email "iamabitbored@innocentdrinks.co.uk" or call the bananaphone. Many people think this must be a bit of a con, yet the reality is that people do drop in, email or phone. These people included a *Financial Times* journalist called Sathnam Sanghera. Cynical journalist as he was (it's part of the training), he suspected that Innocent really could not be as good as they seemed. What would happen if he did just drop in on them for a chat? He would be bound to find evidence to expose them as phoney.

So Sathnam rang the bananaphone, gave a recipe idea and had a nice conversation. But the real test came when he called in early at Fruit Towers, posing as an inquisitive customer. He was invited inside straightaway, offered a smoothie and then given a guided tour by Rowena. His article in the *Financial Times* concluded:

"To my surprise I left the Innocent offices feeling warm and fuzzy. As a customer, I felt valued.
If I'm really honest, I felt more than that: I felt loved.
Indeed, although I started this column by complaining that businesses were getting too touchy-feely, I have now changed my mind. If 'loving' your customers and being 'passionate' means being as generous and open as Innocent, then we all need more love."

It is a very simple way to get feedback: ask for it. Ask for it and mean it. Innocent get hundreds of calls on the bananaphone each week and hundreds of emails. People started ringing from the very first days. The bananaphone (yes, it is) could be answered by anyone at first. Now it rings two or three times on Rowena's or Erin's desk, then it will transfer to anyone to answer. Talking to customers is part of everyone's job and a way to practise being Innocent—and to get better at being Innocent. It is seen as a creative resource for the business. Dan used to answer most of the emails until they got too many for one person.

> "It was one of the best bits ever, being paid to
> e-mail your mates, paid to do what everyone
> does on the sly at work. That was my attitude.
> How would I talk to my mates if they emailed?"

Personal responses to emails continue today. There is a 24-hour deadline for replies and priority is given to people who have had a bad experience. But the vast majority of emails are as Dan describes—mates emailing mates about nothing very much. Except the relationship is cemented, the message is exchanged: "we like each other".

This is how the Innocent tone of voice started to evolve and become stronger day by day. It spread from labels to emails to every part of the business that could be touched by words. When the time came for a "company brochure", Innocent decided to issue its "company rule book". This contains eight rules that are not rules at all, written in the style of naïve, relaxed honesty that is unmistakably Innocent. For example, in the spirit of asking for feedback that began with the yes/no bins and continues with the bananaphone:

The Company Rule Book.

Always ask an expert

What's the answer? We don't know. Most of the time we don't even know the question. But there's always someone we can turn to. And that's you dear reader. We couldn't have done it without you ...

Talking to customers constantly is a good way of staying in touch with reality. The phones continue to ring, emails come pinging in, people drop by. There is no sign of any slackening and there is no intention to discourage it because everyone is now "too busy".

Interesting reading.

Don't believe the hype

We try not to. Don't get us wrong, we've had some lovely things said about us. BBC2 Food & Drink voted us the best smoothie in the UK, and the Independent on Sunday says we're 'the best by far'. We're the 'favourite' health drink of The Sunday Times, and The Express gave us 10 out of 10. Best of all, Fish and Chips International said that we're 'drunk by those in the know'. But we're going to pretend none of it's true—we don't want to get bigheaded or lazy. We just want to produce lovely drinks. And save up enough for a day out at the seaside.

The little square format booklet started making its way around the country, its progress spread by word of mouth. The Innocent company rule book was a distinctive approach to corporate communication. It seemed to say very little, chatting amiably away in a tone that implied "this is no big deal". But the messages sank in.

An apple a day ...

... keeps the doctor away, so imagine what ¾lb of fruit will do. That's the guaranteed minimum amount of fruit used to make each innocent smoothie, which means that just one bottle gives you your recommended daily fruit intake, as well as 150% RDA of natural vitamin C. Our thickies contain probiotic yoghurt cultures to aid digestion, as well as being very low in fat. And our really lovely juices contain two servings of fruit, and are packed full of all sorts of natural nutrients. Professor Millward, Director of the Centre of Nutrition and Food Safety, puts it more succinctly: 'innocent drinks are very good for you'. Doesn't mince his words, that professor.

Innocent has found more and more ways to communicate essentially the same message. It has been able to do this by creating a tone of voice so engaging that you want to read on. On the surface, nothing very much is communicated, but the light touch is deceptive. In 2000, Innocent started sending a weekly newsletter around to friends and contacts. It contained the office gossip—who's just joined, what's happened (normally very little) in the last week—and pieces of real information in the form of trivia. Much of this went onto the website, which itself started to grow and develop features like the online gym: "You can work that body without having to leave your seat." More and more people asked to see the newsletter, and now anyone can subscribe for free to get a weekly dose of Innocent news, gossip, competitions and health tips. "We slip in something occasionally of commercial worth," says Dan. They slipped it to 25,000 people at the beginning of 2006; 100,000 in 2008.

There is a very fine line that Innocent treads on the central issue of health. Everyone is deeply committed to having healthy products that are good for you. At the same time, everyone is deeply concerned not to seem too pompous or preachy about this. Innocent is not full of health freaks or vegan diets. People are simply aware of health issues and wanting to make it easier for anyone to take simple steps to keep healthy: for a start, by having enough fruit. One of the purest and most characteristic Innocent communications is a postcard called "the innocent wee-ometer™". On the back of the card the message is: "Check that you're drinking enough water by using our handy innocent wee-ometer. The darker your wee, the more you need to drink some water." The front of the card has eight oblong blocks of colour, like paint swatches, that range from a pale, almost invisible "I can pee clearly now" through the progressively darker "Half a shandy" and "Beetroot surprise" to the deep orange of "A night out with Keith Richards".

Not everything depends on words. The Innocent visual identity is simple but effective, with the "dude" logo at its heart. Mixing a fruit with a face and an angelic halo, the dude has been an appropriately light-

Family members.

hearted symbol of Innocent since the first days. Other variants sit on other products—the new children's drinks have the logo decorated with other drawings, there are variants of the fruit shape for "detox" and "juicy waters", the cow symbol goes on thickies. The cow vans are one of the most distinctive examples of a corporate transport fleet that you can see. Look out for the cute eyelashes above the headlights and listen for the low mooing sound of the horn.

A cow van.

Recently, Innocent has started advertising on TV, a sure sign of the company's growth. This follows on from the more expected routes of press and outdoor advertising. In some ways it is surprising that Innocent advertises at all, since its growth has been so strong, fuelled by word of mouth recommendation. Yet, with Richard's background in advertising, the move has been a logical one and it has driven even faster growth. Some of the more interesting forms of Innocent advertising have been the more unconventional productions such as the now eagerly awaited Innocent "advent" calendar for January. This is "stuffed full of easy ways to do yourself some good". "Open a window every day and get a little healthy tip." Tips include: "Smile a lot. Monday will seem better"; "One-legged hoovering. See the back of the calendar for instructions"; "Have a smoothie. We sort of had to say that". The calendar is signed off with the message: "Here's to staying healthy the easy way. Innocent smoothies. nothing but nothing but fruit."

Being appointed advertising agency for Innocent could be seen as a dream or a nightmare. How can an ad agency add much to the creativity and understanding of the market that already exists in the business? Ad agencies like to maintain their mystique of superior creativity yet the relationship between Innocent and its agency surely must be different—and perhaps uneasy? Dan explains how it operates.

> "It was tough to find an agency but we chose Lowe. We were strict, we had a defined way of working that included collaboration. We chucked out the traditional way of working. For each ad or campaign we go with a brief that both the agency and Innocent respond to. We'll only go with the best creative solution. And, in smaller print, we said we would only work with an agency that shared our values of sustainability. Lowe have now done a lot in that direction."

This creative approach sounds perfectly plausible until you appreciate that the Innocent team, briefed by Lowe, is Richard and Dan. I saw them two days after they had received the latest creative brief in March.

Stills from a 2006 TV advert.

They were getting ready to compete with the agency's team. The client selection board, to whom the creative teams will pitch their ideas, will consist of Charlotte and Jamie from Innocent. Richard chuckles, "And I'll veto" before insisting "just a joke". This seems an unusual situation but it was the system that produced Innocent's first-ever TV advertising in 2005—in fact, the first UK advertising on TV from a smoothie company. This could not have been simpler, showing smoothie bottles on grass on a sunny day and featuring a voiceover by Dan.

"It was just an extension of the DIY ethic. It was filmed by me, my mates Ed and Henry in the park with a video camera. We tried different voices but people said mine fitted best. I try not to listen. But the advertising worked. We just wanted to get to more people. And we did."

Since then more advertising has come from Innocent. Dan's voice has been replaced by that of Johnny Ball, no doubt a childhood favourite. And they have decided to do the advertising themselves. Dan emphasises Lowe were talented, but Innocent has its own in-house talent so why not do everything?

Dan insists, though, that the label remains the epicentre of the brand's communication strategy. The aim of the advertising is simple, to drive more people to the product and the label. But they considered mass advertising only when distribution of the drinks was national. The label remains the purest form of Innocent, the place where you see best its obsessive attention to detail. Dan sees this as the essential part of his creative role.

"When you stop caring about little Innocent touches, you start thinking like everyone else. We've got lots of clever people here to think about the big stuff. My job is to care about the little stuff. A few days ago we were working on something for Sainsbury's —a point-of-sale card. We invested a day's time in it and we all enjoyed it. It's what our customers expect. They get the extra love and attention to detail. We've had seven years to think the big thoughts: it's fruit, it's healthy. My creative job is just having tiny thoughts, making sure the little stuff stays good."

Ceri Tallett now works with Dan on packaging, particularly to write the labels and the newsletter. A lot is spent on packaging, simply because there are now millions of labels printed, although the printing specifications are simple for bottle labels. The new litre packs are more complex and in full colour, and they have room for much more information. The bottle labels change with a frequency that other companies in this industry could not cope with.

There are 130 different labels produced every quarter. Dan or Ceri writes a brief setting out what Innocent wants to talk about: being natural, the ingredients, specific messages. For each product, for each flavour of smoothie or thickie there is a printing plate that contains eight different labels (or 16 for the most popular products). Each of those has a different story and each word is pored over. Every quarter there is a comedy ingredients session that everyone looks forward to. The writing is mainly in the hands of Dan and Ceri but it is opened out to anyone in the company who wants to join in. It is a massive commitment of time, energy and invention but Innocent know that the label is the finest connection to the loyalty of their consumers.

After a while, you realise just how much this appearance of effortless ease and relaxation is based on intense, hard work. If anything reflects the entrepreneurial spirit it is this. There is a sense of obsession that reminds me of creative agencies, where long days and nights become the norm. What about this image of Innocent people lying around on bean bags? They are obviously working, or perhaps some of them are exhausted. It must be hard to maintain the levels of energy and creativity. How does Dan deal with it?

The labels.

Innocent Pictures and Words department.

"Of course I get stuck. If I do, I stop, come back to it next day. But don't tell Richard. The overnight test is good, just to make sure that the idea is right. Often things look different in the morning. Sometimes you know then exactly what's wrong and what you have to do. A lot of my best stuff I've come back to after three or four months—you park them, live with the ideas. A word or a first line can then unlock it."

"Rich and I will sit down, revisiting an old idea. We've already had lots of the big ideas, so we're making sure we take care of the details. But there's loads to come in terms of products and new stuff. The passion is still there. I can't overstress how passionate everyone is about the business and what an advantage that is. I want to make sure that Number 104 feels that just as much as Number 4. The most important creative resource we have is the people indoors. If there are great people here, I'll always have ideas. You just ask them and you get ideas."

"It started like this and it doesn't feel any different now. We've just gone from 20 cases to thousands, but that doesn't mean we need to change approach. It's like being passionate about your kids—if you're there for the birth, you're attached to it."

Dan is the proud new father of baby Ruby but he is still very proud of Innocent. New daughter Violet has just arrived, so he's now even prouder. He was once tempted away but decided that a glamorous new lifestyle overseas would not compensate for the family at Innocent. Dan is not one of the founders yet he shares the founding zeal. So, crucially, do other members of the team. The result is a whole string of awards that recognise Innocent's business skills, its creativity and the quality of its products. There is a lot to be proud of.

Poster, 2003 advertising.

Mangoes & Passion Fruits.

Top of the Pops

(20 of the best Innocent labels selected by John Simmons, Dan Germain and Pan's People led by Ceri Tallett)

Well I never. The family just keeps growing.

We started off with three little 'uns. Then along came mangoes and passionfruits. Well, to be honest, he was a bit unexpected. We put it down to that anniversary trip to Dorset. Now, just as we'd got a people carrier to hold the four of them, up pops blackberries and blueberries. She's a feisty one, just like her mum.

Another mouth to feed—I just don't know where the money's going to come from. If you can help, email shoesforthekids@freshtrading.co.uk

Four years ago, life was very different. Innocent hadn't really got off the ground, Christina Aguilera was doing the dishes down at the Wimpy bar in Mexico City, and the spoon was still just an idea on an inventor's drawing board. Thankfully, things have come on in leaps and bounds since then. The spoon has become part of everyday life, Christina has rocked our world, and we have provided lots of people with their recommended daily intake of fruit in a bottle. Who would have thought it?

It's great to get back to nature. But instead of taking off your clothes and running down the high street, why not 'become' a fruit? To achieve this, put some weird floaty music on, lie down, relax and say to yourself, "I am an apple. I am an apple, I feel the wind brush against me as I hang in the tree." In no time at all, you'll find that the worries of the day melt away, and your only concern will be whether you're about to be turned into a pie.

Lost Property
We found all of these after our Fruitstock
Festival in August—a set of house keys, a pair
of reading specs, a few pairs of sunglasses and
a pretty dress.

If any of them belong to you, please ring the banana
phone on 020 8600 3939 as soon as possible,
as all of it technically becomes ours in 3 months' time
and Jon is really looking forward to getting his hands
on the dress.

In the olden days people lived in trees and wore
dresses made of mud. But they probably had a healthier
diet than us. Nuts for breakfast, berries for lunch and
maybe a special treat of seared pterodactyl steaks for
dinner. Following the olden days people's lead, we
thought we'd keep things old-fangled, by putting nothing
but your recommended daily intake of fruit in a bottle.
Guaranteed pterodactyl-free.

Sometimes it's the simple things that make you happy.
Waking up on a sunny morning. Folding a map correctly
the first time. Beating your Mum at arm wrestling. Or just
drinking a smoothie. Our smoothies contain only the purest
and freshest fruit. No concentrates, preservatives or additives
of any kind. And they're made and delivered daily.
We could try to make it more complicated but that would
mean less time to sleep and eat. Two more simple things
that we hold dear.

My mum grows too much stuff on her allotment.
She sends me down big padded envelopes full of runner
beans after she's harvested her crop. It's magic, because
I can never bring myself to throw them away, so I have
to invent new dishes. Runner bean Bolognese. Runner bean
burgers. Runner beans a l'orange. Anyway, the moral
of the story is that there's no one way to get more fruit
and veg into your diet. There are a million ways, including
this smoothie. And an envelope full of runner beans.

Hello. If you're reading this then you must be bored.
Still, there's never anything good on TV anymore
is there? Magnum PI, now that was a programme
worth watching.

Anyway, this juice is made from fruit and nothing
else. Like Magnum, we've no time for baddies;
that means no concentrates, no GM foods and no
additives whatsoever. We just crush the best fruit
into bottles and get them to you as quickly as possible.

Sounds easy, tastes delicious.

We've worked really hard to make the best drinks
since we sold our first smoothies on April 28th 1999.
And we had to forego some stuff in order to make
things a success—sleep, a regular social life, shoes that fit,
a proper breakfast etc. But we're doing a bit better these
days when it comes to our work-life balance, and some
mornings you'll find us having a leisurely sausage platter
on the Uxbridge Road before walking to work in nice
new comfortable shoes. There are some things you just
can't put a price on.

Do you ever mistakenly buy eggs instead of lychees?
Never fear—we've written a guide to help you spot
the difference, just in case. Firstly, lychees have pink
shells and come in bunches, whereas eggs have brown
shells and come in boxes with pictures of chickens on
them. Lychees taste nice in smoothies like this one,
whereas Eggs taste nice with soldiers, We reckon that
should be enough information for now, but if you have any
problems, give us a ring on the banana phone and we'll
help you buy the right thing.

innocent

Innocent smoothies contain only the purest and Freshest
fruit. No concentrates, preservatives or additives of any
kind. And they're made and delivered daily. Now that's
out of the way I'm using this space for a personal message:
Brian, if you're reading this, do you want to come to the
zoo next Thursday? My boss is on a training thing, so it's
all cool. They've opened the new penguin bit and apparently
one of the pandas is expecting. I've taped this wing mirror
to a stick so you won't have to stand on a box or
wear those tall shoes or anything. Call me.

We have global aspirations. We want to make
the best smoothies in the whole world, ever.
That means one thing. Getting the best fruit in the
whole world, ever. Which explains why we use
Alphonso mangoes from India, Smooth Cayenne
pineapples from Costa Rica and Valencia oranges
from Jamaica.

We're not doing it because we want to go to
glamorous foreign places. We're doing it so
we get the best fruit. I mean, our strawberries
come mainly from Poland and you wouldn't go
there unless you had to, would you?

Noses, eggs and ice rinks. All rubbish when
they are runny. We much prefer things nice
'n' thick, which is why we've made this thickie.

If you wade through it you'll realise it contains
live probiotic yoghurt, fruit, honey and absolutely
Nothing else—no sugar, no additives, no nothing.

And, best of all, the yoghurt is very low in fat,
ensuring that while our thickies will always
remain thick, you can carry on being thin.

Under advice from the lawyers of a Ms M Nature,
We have been forced to issue the following:

"We, innocent, agree to stop claiming responsibility
for the wonderful fruit contained inside this bottle. We
understand that the fact our drinks taste nice has nothing
to do with us. All we do is gather up fruit, crush it and
put it into bottles. Furthermore, we apologise for any
confusion you may have suffered."

Fruit™ is the registered trademark of Mother Nature.

Van Gogh. Tolstoy. Manilow. They get better with every
passing year, allowing each new generation to discover
their wonders. So it gives us great pride to add this recipe
to that list. It's always been our most popular recipe, and
we've just made it a bit better. You see, it now has three
extra strawberries in it. Three of the plump little chaps.
They make it look a bit pinker and more importantly they
make it taste even better. Superlative. Timeless. One
of the greats. Add it to your collection immediately.

Dear Mum. Yes we know everyone else's kids are now
qualified lawyers and getting married to the daughter of
someone who owns a castle, but we're doing OK too.
Why, just the other day we found a way of improving on
this thickie. No mean feat. We've found a new creamy,
low-fat, West country yoghurt, and the result is pretty
special. We know you'll be tempted to boast about
our achievements to your friends, but remember, not
everyone's children have had the opportunity to make such
important advances in the field of yoghurt-based drinks.

You can tell if a pineapple is ready to eat by sniffing its
bottom (it should smell all ripe and pineappley). And seeing
as sniffing bottoms in public is a rare treat, it's worth
having a go. Sure, you might get a few funny looks in the
supermarket. And the manager might ask you to leave
the store for interfering with tropical fruit. But then again,
you'll be one going home with a tasty ripe pineapple for
your tea. PS please remember to stick to pineapples.

innocent

To all the people with moustaches. To all the people with
red cars and blue cars and even the lady with the yellow
car (it was going cheap). To all the people with too much
homework, and those with wobbly teeth and crocheted
blankets. To all of those who sleep late, sleep early and
go to the shops to buy crisps in the night. To all the people
who want to get more fruit into their lives – this one's
for you. It tastes good and it'll do you good. We hope it
makes your day a little better than it was before, and if
you need anything else, you know where we are. Just call.

Acai. Pronounced "ass-eye-eeee". Say it out loud: *ass eye
eee, aah-sye-heeee*. Shout it before you pull off a plaster
or as you administer a devastating karate chop to the
kingpin of crime. Maybe though, because acai berries are
ridiculously good for you, you could say it after sneezing
or when greeting someone, to bring them good fortune.
But woe betide them if they take the mick out of your
new moustache. That's when pure karate kicks in. Be like
water making its way through cracks. Be water my friend.

... and step away from the desk 2 3 4, come on, really
work it ... now, off to the shops, oh yes, keep those
knees up, keep it working 2 3 4 ... stop at the lights,
mind the cyclist ... and into the shop, just grab the
bottle 2 3 4 ... feel it in the triceps, oh yeah ... you're
feeling good now ... stepping to the till, ignore the
chocolate, keep stepping, let's see those glutes shake
2 3 4 ... and we'll finish with the 'unscrew', pop
those wrists 2 3 4 ... looking good ... and relax ...

Chapter Four

Be Generous

*The main factor is "Are you a nice person?"
There's not one person in Innocent I wouldn't
spend a Saturday afternoon with. It comes from
taking recruitment seriously."*

Brontë Blomhoj

The awards shown in the previous chapter demonstrate a great range but it is significant that some of them have been given for Innocent's enlightened approach as an employer. It's good to win creative awards, prizes for product quality and recognition for fast growth, but it is unusual for a new, small company to be credited as "Top Employer of the Year—2005". Winning awards takes a bit of luck but there is nothing accidental in the kind of awards that a company wins. Generally, you win categories that matter to the company, where real effort has been put in to grow the company's reputation. Winning awards for looking after its people matters to Innocent, perhaps more than it does to other companies. Awards and rewards are built into the way Innocent thinks of itself as a brand. "Be generous," it advises, "with rewards when people deliver". There is a culture of support and praise for people, starting with "be nice to each other".

This particular company value about generosity is centred on Innocent's people, so in this chapter I will be exploring how Innocent relates to its own people through those actions and policies that come under "P & E"—people and environment. By putting the two together rather than the more usual and heartless sounding "human resources"—Innocent acknowledges that providing the right space in which to work is a crucial aspect of recruiting and keeping the best people. But environment is not simply seen as space, the physical buildings and offices, but the right conditions in which people can flourish.

First of all, meet Rowena. When I meet Rowena, she has almost lost her voice to a sore throat. Although her voice is unusually croaky that day she is very happy to speak to me. Indeed she is very happy. Rowena is one of those people who makes you feel happier just by talking to you, which qualifies her to be the "People's Champion", following in the footsteps of Dan Germain.

Rowena first started drinking the drinks. She was based in the north-west of England and came across Innocent smoothies here and there. Occasionally, she saw the cow vans and she picked up a copy of the "innocent company rule book" in a Lake District café. After that, she visited the website frequently and enjoyed the online gym. She thought "they seem to care about people" so she sent in her CV in hope not expectation. The reply came back that they would keep her details on file. This turned out to be more than the usual fobbing-off device when she was afterwards called in to talk about a job. Rowena thinks that her suggestion of a chat room on the website helped her stand out.

So it was that Rowena became Number 14 and Office Squeeze. On her first day she brought Kendal Mint Cake from home. As it was a Monday she was plunged straight into the Monday morning meeting where she found everyone relaxed and friendly but just a bit daunting.

> "They all knew each other, they were like mates with their in-jokes. But soon you're in yourself anyway so it doesn't matter. I listened to everyone talking about what they were doing then joined in the exercise at the end. My personal favourite exercise is sleeping lions."

Rowena worked with Dan to reply to emails and to be the main voice of the bananaphone. Innocent had always been keen to create relationships with consumers that went beyond the "customer satisfaction survey". Asking people to ring or write is a simple way of getting

Rowena on the bananaphone.

feedback but everyone was surprised at just how many consumers responded. Rowena describes her job like this:

> "Every day's different. Look at the inbox, answer complaints, answer different kinds of emails, answer letters (from kids with drawings to 80-year-old ladies). Meet people who drop in. Answer the bananaphone, sing a song, recite a poem."

Rowena explains that people ring up the bananaphone then sometimes hang up in surprise when they hear a real voice. It's still so unusual in business to say ring up/drop in and mean it that many people expect a recorded message or a façade like the *Wizard of Oz* where you'll discover the whole set-up is run by a charlatan. We are trained now to be cynical. Innocent's transparent innocence can be disconcerting. But when you have tested it out (like the FT journalist) and discovered that it is real, the effect is to increase your belief in and loyalty towards the brand.

A few years into the job, Rowena had extra responsibilities. She was asked to run HR although she had no HR background. When the number of employees grew to 40, she became the People's Champion and Innocent started to get a little more seriously professional about HR. Rowena left because she wanted to return to the north to be near her family, and she did a mind-numbing job that was obviously nothing like her role in Innocent. After a while she asked "Can I come back and have some creativity again? And can I stay up north?" This led to the setting up of the Manchester office, with other members of the sales team who are northern-based. Because the office is above a fishmongers, they call it Fish Towers. Rowena pops down to London weekly. She brings a story or two down with her as well as Kendal Mint Cake. For example ...

A lady wrote in, describing the mangoes and passion fruits smoothie as golden nectar. She had a golden wedding coming up so Rowena arranged for some smoothies to be sent to her. The lady then got in touch again to say "I'd love it if you came to our anniversary party". What do you do? Rowena drove to Nottingham to be at the party. Everyone in Fruit Towers wrote in the card and someone wrote "Row has a beautiful voice". When this was read at the party Rowena was in demand to perform a song. Did she ever get to sing at the party? Rowena's not saying but she'll tell you the party was great.

Rowena cheerfully admits to singing on the banana-phone, though. It's part of being upbeat and friendly with everyone. The bananaphone will be answered by Rowena or Erin on the first two or three rings, then it will switch to be answered by anyone. Everyone takes a turn at answering the bananaphone and at Christmas time there are even group efforts, with people singing carols. Rowena says: "You get over the fact that you feel silly. As long as we keep doing these things, we'll take on the big boys."

Taking on the big boys. Innocent call it the Pepsi Challenge since the American corporation acquired PJ's. There is a part of Innocent that still needs to pinch itself at its own growth. It has become the UK's fastest growing company in the food and drink business. It still sees itself as a small company but this cannot last for much longer. Yet there is no reason why Innocent should change the way it thinks or behaves as a brand. It remains, and should remain, focused on small, essential details and creating relationships between people without the weight of the corporate hand on the keyboard.

It comes down to the quality of Innocent's people and the relationship between them and the brand. Recruiting people to Innocent can look haphazard from the outside —"try accountancy to start but switch to writing labels if you prefer"—but it is extremely rigorous. It goes beyond "Is he/she a nice person?" to considering (sometimes at great length) whether people will fit in, have exceptional skills and can add something unusual. I met Brontë from P & E, who joined three years earlier from Goldman Sachs. She had seen a job on the Innocent website that said "we need someone to take care of us". To apply she sent in a transcript of the first interview so they could "go straight to the second one when we first met". She was called in for interviews. "All the boys are from consultancies so they ask logic questions like 'Why are manhole covers round?'"

Once you're in, Innocent believes in proper welcomes. As she walked in there was a big sign saying "Welcome Brontë". People get flowers on their first day and they are shown to their seat which is invariably next to someone doing a completely different job. People do not sit in departments. Brontë sat next to Ed the designer. As the company gets bigger (it had more than 100 people when we were talking), space becomes more of an issue. Fruit Towers will not win architectural awards but it has its own style that people wish to maintain, and no-one wants the company to be on split sites.

"We want the environment to be home with a few more computers. People work hard but there are relaxing aspects. If we had more space, we would add more relaxation. A lot of our current attention is going towards expanding the space—here, if we can. We've had Astroturf on the floors, and the walls even, from the first day. It's cheap as carpet but more Innocent. We have more and more hot desks and people work from home if they want to."

Brontë is known as Queen Bee, a title you can probably work out for yourself. Innocent titles can be a little arch, and I doubt if one of the founders actually introduces himself to a potential supplier as Chief Squeezer. They establish a unique style, though, and most of them have an appropriateness that makes you smile. Ailana who runs PR is known as Juice Press, people in accounts are Big Spender and Miss Moneypenny. It works internationally too as Innocent develops. You might guess that Windmill Warrior and a Clogwork Orange are two of the Dutch team. Brontë herself is from Denmark. When I emailed her, I got the following "out of office reply".

Hejsa.

Somewhere, beyond the sea, is a small country called Denmark. It's almost like a fairy tale there: lots of little castles set amongst the rolling green hills, beautiful princes and princesses who ride white horses around town, their blonde shiny hair shimmering like gold on the gentle minus 15 degree breeze. Happy people are Danish people who love nothing more than to wave red and white flags around profusely—and drink what is probably the best beer in the world. They also love not saying the word "please" but we can't be too upset about this, for in this lovely country, a word for "please" simply does not exist. Truly, a magical (but sometimes a little bit rude) place.

So, I've gone to the Wonderful Copenhagen for a few days. I'll be running around going to lots of important meetings and it is unlikely I'll be on e-mail (no fancy Berry thing for me, but my mobile is on so you can try to catch me that way if you need to get hold of me).

Alternatively, you can contact Clarissa@innocentdrinks.co.uk if it is urgent. She's not Danish and is extremely polite.

Bye for now (or hej-hej, as the Danes would say).

Brontë

Although Brontë and Dan are clearly different kinds of people, there is enough similarity to convince you that they speak for the same brand. That is a difficult feat to pull off but Innocent does not try to impose guidelines issued by the tone of voice police. They simply trust their own people to be Innocent, to have absorbed the brand's fundamental character. But clearly you need the right people.

"We find them and they find us," Brontë explains. "People go to the website to look for jobs, or they read something in the newsletter. We also offer £1,000 headhunting fee if our people recommend a friend who gets a job. Then we also advertise a little in the specialist press if we're looking for someone with very specific skills."

The jobs pages of the Innocent website will tell you that the company is serious about this area. It is worth reading the careers section to get a measure of Innocent the brand. Although there is much here that reminds you of the tone from the smoothie labels, there is no doubt that these people think hard about their business in all its details—and they want to get things right.

How we work at innocent
We're a team of committed, ambitious, hardworking people who have an altruistic and realistic view of the world. We work hard, but we ensure that everyone shares in the resulting rewards, and we give people the opportunity to develop themselves and to be part of something they can be proud of. We want people of all ages, and from diverse cultural backgrounds, and, most importantly, we want people who inspire and deliver change around them. If this sounds like the sort of workplace you want to contribute to then please email www.innocentdrinks.co.uk/bored/jobs/positions_available.html to check out our vacancies.

And if you fancy applying please follow the guidelines we have set out. Please do follow them, otherwise we can't get back in touch. We apologise if this all sounds a bit serious, but while working at innocent is informal and enjoyable, we do take the people side of things seriously.

How to apply
We ask everyone to write us a letter to send in along with their full CV. It's a bit like an interview before the interview, really. Please keep the letter to one page only. It should briefly cover the following five topics:

Your reasons for wanting to work at innocent and the role in question—why this job, and innocent right for you? We love people who create change and leave things better than they find them, so briefly tell us about a situation in your work or personal life where you took the initiative and made something happen. Tell us about a problem you solved recently. What was the issue and what was your solution? We're looking for people that take on challenges and sort them out. Again, this could be from your work or personal life. What are you passionate about? You should also send your most up to date CV, making sure you put details of your previous work experience as well as information about exams and grades. Add legal hobbies if you so wish. Once you're done, send your application by email to: jobs@innocentdrinks.co.uk

You can also send your application along with the postman, to:

A job would be nice
innocent drinks
Fruit Towers
3 Goldhawk Estate
Brackenbury Road
London W6 0BA

We're really sorry, but because we want to give all of our attention to people who make an effort, we can't respond unless you take the time to write us a letter as outlined above. Although bribes in the form of chocolates and home baked cakes are, as always, greatly appreciated. We promise to share.

Bye for now.

When I interview Dan Shrimpton and Daisy together, it becomes clear that Innocent has changed a lot while remaining fundamentally the same. Daisy now runs trade communications but originally (she is Number 6) she was general help with everything—both PA and van driver. She has grown into her current role.

Dan (Number 25) joined three years in. He used to work in the City, and he loved drinking Innocent smoothies. One day his smoothie was unpleasantly fizzy so he wrote to complain, while taking the opportunity to attach his CV. He was interviewed and offered a job in the accounts team of two. After two years as an Innocent accountant, during which time he wrote some labels because he enjoyed it, he became communications manager in the marketing team. In a small business you get exposed to all the other work and you can move towards your own areas of interest. Some of that might be seeping out of Innocent but it is still a remarkably flexible workplace.

That, of course, is one reason why people want to work there. Generally, though, it is just perceived as a nice place to be, mainly because of the people. As Daisy puts it:

> "The people make Innocent special, from the three founders on. You want to work hard because you want the business to succeed for them. People really believe in it, the brand has such an honesty, a genuine soul. Innocent is the magnet for like-minded people, they're great at identifying people who get it. It's such a human brand, people relate to it."

Generosity shows in the way Innocent will say thank you, not just with words but with smoothies and other gifts. Sensing this, or perhaps as a result of experiencing it, people send messages in bottles, cakes, chocolates, presents of all kinds. Sometimes it works, and there are stories of people getting jobs after such approaches, but inevitably most of the time it does not. The cake was still nice, to send and to eat. Innocent has become expert at dealing with criticism, complaints and bad news. As much effort goes into rejection letters as letters of appointment—whereas most companies give little attention to either. Here is a rejection letter:

Hello Peter

Thanks a million for sending us your CV and letter—it was really good to hear from you. Unfortunately, the opportunities we have at the business are not really Peter-shaped. You have some great skills and some really interesting experience, but I am afraid that right now, we are not able to take things further. We know that's not the nicest thing to hear, but we're still a small business and growing lots—maybe in the future, the picture looks a bit different: keep up to date on all the developments through our newsletter and website (we advertise our roles there first). Everybody at fruit towers wishes you all the best and hopes you find the perfect opportunity for you very soon.

Bye for now.

I suspect that any rejection letter causes a little wave of resentment inside. The hope is simply to contain the negative feeling. As the recipient, naturally, of many "Dear John" letters, I'm not sure that talk of the lack of John-shaped opportunity would soften the blow or make me grind my teeth. On the other hand, the letter of appointment and employment contract must be a joy to read. You have a job and the confirmation of that job is written in a way that affirms your attraction to the Innocent brand in the first place. The contract is legal (and confidential) but it manages to convey the essential information—including stuff about discipline—in a tone of voice that is recognisably that of the brand.

It is vital to get the right people and then to give them clarity of purpose. A large part of that is to do with being very clear about what the company and the brand stand for. Innocent is in the fortunate position of attracting people who have an intuitive understanding of the brand anyway. The situation is completely opposite to that on the TV series *The Apprentice*, when the final contestants were asked the most basic questions about Sir Alan

Innocent sampling.

Sugar's company. What does Amstrad do? What does it stand for? The contestants did not have a clue.

Such things matter to Innocent. Generosity needs to flow two ways, and it goes with an openness and honesty in personal relationships that also happen to be working relationships. The divide between working life and personal life is not a vast chasm, as in some companies; the self you bring to work needs to be close to the self that is you outside work. The framework of HR best practice—open dialogue, six-monthly assessments etc—is there, but it is a more natural part of the way people work.

The whole relationship between employer and employee has any hint of confrontation removed. Simply doing things together, having fun together inside and outside work, is what Innocent does. A night out as a group is not arranged with a feeling of angst; office perks are not special treats from the management; company trips away are not arranged with measurable team-building objectives. Just have fun.

Here are some of the things that Innocent does in that spirit, and most of these have happened since the earliest days. The whole company goes away for an annual break. This started as a skiing and snowboarding trip, growing out of the fact that Richard, Adam and Jon took their winter holidays together in the Alps. As the company got bigger it became clear that not everyone loved skiing: 60 people went to Switzerland, everyone enjoyed the après-ski but only 20 skied. So the ski trip has now metamorphosed into a Nature Weekend that happens every year—and involves a little more luxury than the name might lead you to expect. That is the fixed highpoint of a fun-loving culture. There are film evenings and informal parties that happen more spontaneously because the weather's nice or they fancy a beer. If it's summer there are lots of picnics. Ailana organises a monthly Cheese Club where people try different kinds of cheese. There is a summer sports day in Ravenscourt Park, a mix of adrenaline activities and leisurely gentle ones. None of these activities prevents work being done by the end of the week. Perhaps they are now undertaken with slightly more awareness of purpose. People talk about the need to make more of an effort to keep it a small, friendly company as it gets bigger. But this can simply mean that people sometimes do things together in groups rather than as the whole company. Even as some people worry about the dangers of getting bigger, they still make observations like: "If I get grumpy (we all do sometimes) I think of other places I've worked". The effort to keep everyone feeling part of the same venture, sharing the same destiny, pays off.

The activities described in the previous paragraphs are mainly about people enjoying their place of work and their colleagues. There is no direct connection between work and reward, although it is obviously there by implication. If Innocent made no money, there would be no Nature Weekends. But there are many activities designed to help people feel more fulfilled and to reward hard work and commitment. A little thing—Innocent loves to have lots of little things to make the big thing as rich as possible—is the Lord or Lady of the Sash. This is awarded once a month "for services to fruit" (as the sash says). The winners get tea made for them for a month. Rather more substantial but in a similar spirit, there are Innocent scholarships. Anyone in the company can apply to win a £1,000 scholarship to do something life-affirming that they really want to do. Scholarships are awarded every three months. The first scholarship

The innocent Nature Weekend.

of 2006 was won by Andrew who is going to climb Mount Kilimanjaro. Before him, Kate went to Sri Lanka to help clean up after the tsunami; Pete fulfilled his dream of having a fresh water fish tank; and Alexis recorded a demo-CD.

The business case for doing this is to do with staff retention, but the brand value "be generous" drives the business case. Other companies might approach an issue like staff retention in a completely different way, without reference to the brand, because in those cases the brand is an artificially imposed construct. In Innocent it is a natural part of everything that happens, and there is a realisation that the brand really lives through its people.

Lord of the Sash

You have to look after your people not simply to retain them and reduce the costs of staff turnover, but to help them perform at their best. If they perform at their best the company will thrive and grow. But you have to make sure that everyone understands what is going on, how your work as an individual relates to that of your colleagues and where you are all headed. A lot of effort is given to making sure that the business is transparent and that everyone feels connected. The Monday morning meetings always happen, driven by a spirit of sharing information but delivered with pace and humour. Yet they are full of hard information, facts and figures.

Once a quarter, this information-sharing gets extended to a company meeting. The meetings are for everyone and they had always been held in Fruit Towers until, in March 2006, there was simply not enough room to hold all the people—more than 100—then in the company. I met Richard in February when this problem was looming but that day he was excited because he had discovered a great place to hold the company meeting. Strangely enough it was the same unusual-looking building that I had asked Dan about when walking past it earlier in the day. Dan had never been in it, but now Richard had. By the time I saw him again in April, the company meeting had taken place in the building, which is actually a church, and had been judged a success. But I know that for Richard what really clinched it, what told him that this was meant to be, was the name—the Church of the Holy Innocents.

They used the church, holding the meeting in a beautiful room in the rafters, with light pouring in through the stained glass that ran from floor to ceiling. They covered the floor in grass and bean bags, transforming the setting into an Innocent space. All the same, it was an unusual setting to be discussing ways the company was tackling its five main initiatives:

Recruiting and developing talent
Taking on Pepsi
Pushing into Europe
Launching the kids' drinks
Sustainability

The presentations, using slides, are followed by a question and answer session when the founders answer any questions, sent in anonymously in advance. Everyone is treated as an intelligent adult able to understand all areas of the business—or at least as wishing to understand them. It is a philosophy shared by all the founders. As Adam put it:

"Everyone should have input to strategic questions. It's just an extension of sitting around on a beanbag on a Friday night, thinking about where you want the business to go next. People's views are important. We have to take the views of consumers and customers, but of our people too."

The latest company meetings have been held in the Lyric Theatre, Hammersmith, but the aim is still to involve as much as possible. Chatwich has the same aim. Richard winces a little at the name but the Chatwich sessions have been running since the beginning of 2006. What more can the employer of the year do? Clearly it has to keep moving forward and finding new ways to grow without losing its soul. By the end of 2005, Innocent had grown 130 per cent in a year and taken on 40 new people. This was a big growth spurt, underlining the need for everyone to be sharing the same vision—and the value of new ideas coming from anyone. The

Chatwich sessions—a lunchtime chat with a sandwich—are intended to do just that. The only difference is that now, in mid-2008, Innocent employs 270 people, 160 of them at Fruit Towers.

> "The number of great ideas that come up in just one lunchtime session can be phenomenal— some ideas are already being put into place, while others, such as Innocent naked camping, are a little further down the list."

The Chatwich discussions have been on finance, new products, Fruitstock, the Innocent Foundation. No subject is ruled out; everyone is encouraged to contribute ideas. Anyone can ask anything anytime—or, if they wish, they can use an Innocent question card. It is all part of building an intelligent culture that aspires constantly to do things better. Richard is very clear about why they want to do this.

> "Open communication within a company not only makes everyone feel that their opinions are genuinely appreciated and valued, but, by taking the time to catch up once in a while over a few smoothies and a sandwich, we can also emphasise that everyone in our business can have an influence on what we are doing and where we want to go next."

Innocent starts from a base of highly intelligent people. They are also people who want to develop their intelligence and skills. The Innocent Academy was recently established to help people do that. But, of course, it is run in a distinctively Innocent way. There is a fundamental belief in Innocent that the best way to learn is to teach. The person on the receiving end of teaching benefits but so too does the person delivering the teaching. The teachers have to think through what

The Chatwich sessions/Scandinavia Day.

they do. So the Innocent Academy is designed to use the knowledge and skills of Innocent people to teach other Innocent people. The belief is that everyone in the building has something that they do better than anyone else—so let's use that expertise, passing on tips, being generous with time.

People get taken away for two days for training sessions "in a nice hotel with great baths". There are peer groups who work with a leader, with modules of leadership, strategic thinking, negotiating, personal effectiveness and presentation skills. The best people in the building are chosen for each module—and for new ones that will be developed. These trainers are then combined with outside experts from the London Business School. The aim is for everyone to pass through the Innocent Academy.

There is enormous support and, as you might imagine, enormous pressure. One Oxford graduate (there is a very high proportion of Oxbridge graduates at Innocent) likened joining Innocent to arriving at that university.

"Before arriving you'd been top of the class, now you're not. It can lead to a crisis of confidence. We have real over-achievers here. But no-one is trying to put one over on anyone. Everyone helps. There is an Oxbridge influence but it's egalitarian —that's not a contradiction if you've been there."

The harshest thing you might find to say about working at Innocent is that it is a very competitive environment. It does not necessarily show as a pressure to score points or to prove that you are better than someone else. It comes out in ways that should be seen as strengths. For example, there is a tone of voice, a language that people pick up. Everyone—without exception—speaks enthusiastically about the brand. But, of course, there are Innocent ways of doing that. It starts with the basics of saying "hello" or "hi" to be personable. There are Innocent phrases, almost subconscious. "Today it's all about ..." is one. There is an enjoyable sense of competition, to bring things to life with words. This comes naturally to Richard, Dan and others but probably puts a little pressure on others who do not have quite the same facility to be as articulate or funny.

Richard is aware of the need to reduce pressure. It seems to work with Dan because you could not imagine anyone more relaxed. And Dan spreads his calm to others. But Richard recognises that the pressure needs to be released and this is why the work hard/play hard ethic is always strong. The current obsession was to do with being busy. Richard recognises that everyone is too busy and the reality is that they cannot do the to-do list; as a result people leave work knowing that there is still more to do, and this creates more stress. The response is to say OK, you cannot do everything, so spend time on the actions that really create impact. Agree with your team leader what are the top three things you should do, write them down. When you are busy, do the most important things first.

It is a humanitarian and practical approach. There is no pressure created by penalties for not meeting targets. The pressure comes from people wanting to do well and wanting to work hard because they believe in the cause. People who work in Innocent do see it as a cause, and they are proud to work there. They know that their friends are envious, bored with the jobs they do elsewhere. Hard work is its own reward, but in Innocent hard work is also rewarded. After a year of service, everyone gets a small stake in the company and there is profit sharing. If the profits are good (they have been so far) people get a bonus worth something like 15 per cent of salary. And Innocent gives ten per cent of its profits to charity through its own Foundation.

It is a spirit of generosity, admirable in a modern business. Most portrayals of business are nothing like Innocent, but most businesses are nothing like Innocent. On the morning that I wrote this, after the conclusion of *The Apprentice* on TV the previous night, there was a discussion on BBC radio's Today programme. Sir Alan Sugar had portrayed a ruthless businessman, driven by results and financial targets, operating in a harshly competitive dog-eat-dog environment. It was gripping television but it did not present business life in the kindest light. The question posed by Today was, "Does business have to be ruthless?" Today had obviously sought an antidote to the Sugar way, and they had come up with Innocent and Adam Balon to put an alternative view. Adam's view was simply, "It's much better to be nice to each other".

All over the UK, people on their way to work probably had a smoothie to celebrate.

Innocent, August 2004.

Chapter Five

Be Commercial

Our bottle supplier dropped us when they got a bigger contract. You try to learn from these things. What did we learn? Get two bottle suppliers.

Adam Balon

Richard has an engaging habit of musing in a conversation. It makes you feel as if he is thinking a fresh thought that he wants to share with you—in that spirit of innocent generosity. It is a trait that runs through the company. Sometimes people muse and say not very much but it's OK because they didn't promise to be deep. There is a lack of portentousness about Innocent. They strive hard, they succeed, they grow but they never give the impression of being fixated by achieving future commercial goals. It makes them seem unbusinesslike to many on the outside but that is an impression they are happy to live with. It disarms the competition and they are certainly commercial enough to worry about the competition. Richard muses: "There's something about being altruistic but being allowed to be commercial."

The thought is about Innocent winning permission and the right to be commercial because people trust it to do good things. That kind of trust is rare in the business world. Yet we should not see Innocent as a group of friends who are in business simply to have a good time and be nice to people. They want to do good but they have to earn money first. "Hippies with calculators" is one description that is quoted by Innocent people. Maurice Pinto says they do things right but they also do the right things.

The brand value "be commercial" is not an afterthought. There was not a sudden realisation "we'd better make some money too". The founders were always very clear that Innocent would be a business and therefore it needed to make profits. They believed, though, that they could do that if they persuaded people to like them first, and to like them for what they did. But the injunctions that underpin the brand value are focused enough on business to appeal to Sir Alan Sugar.

Create growth and profit for us and customers. Be tough, but fair. Think clearly, act decisively and keep the main thing, the main thing.

The view of a brand from inside is always different from outside. Innocent people are wonderful ambassadors for the brand. But Innocent consumers have also been champions for the brand. We have looked a lot at the inside view, how things developed, how they are. A large part of Innocent's commercial success, however, has been its ability to get consumers to engage with its story. Which then makes it easier for customers—meaning the retailers, large and small—to buy from Innocent. The Innocent story has had the advantage of becoming legendary in the marketing and creative industries, and people from these industries are the best placed and the best-qualified to tell a brand's story by word of mouth. There has always been a buzz about Innocent, fuelled by the professional creative world, as shown below.

Why do you like innocent?

"I like the fact that Innocent Drinks was started by people from ads who understood the value of a simple idea executed well. I like this more than the product itself which I rarely buy. I like stories like Ben & Jerry, Innocent, Pret (Julian Metcalf in particular) because they stay close to being real businesses rather than processed ones."
–Tony Allen, Fortune Street (ex MD, Interbrand)

"From a personal point of view because they make great smoothies; and from a professional point of view because they make the sceptical believe in the difference that clever, honest branding can make. They generally just make the world more interesting."
–Rob Williams, Creative Director, Penguin Books

"They are fun, interesting and appear to mean
what they say. They reinforce my belief in
instinct and in the power of tone of voice."
–Andy Milligan, brand consultant,
author of *See, Feel, Think, Do*

"Most importantly, they are good drinks (especially
the Detox Super Smoothie). But they also feel like a
bit of a gang I wouldn't mind being part of. I like
their sense of humour, and the words from the labels
give me (I believe) a good idea of what they're like."
–Neil Taylor, Creative Director, The Writer

Will Awdry is a renowned figure in advertising who has
observed their progress. He heads the creative work at
DDB, which has not worked with Innocent, and is now
moving on to another advertising giant, Ogilvy, so he
has no need to look at Innocent through rose-tinted
glasses. His views are considered.

"In an oxymoronic way, Innocent exploded gently
into my life thanks to its extraordinary reasonableness.
I discovered it as a juice drinker rather than as an
advertising man. However, the brand now runs through
the veins of the ad business as an inspirational elixir
of great communication. It is much talked about
but—so far—has been copied by few others.

"I like Innocent because the juices, smoothies,
other products and the language employed
to sell them are all delicious.

"Innocent was born eloquent. It is a brand that—
genuinely—talks with its customers not to, or at them.
This is a reflection of the mastery of great writing.
Like those nurses who talk to mute patients and yet
who keep it conversational, Innocent's approach to
customers has a two-way element. It balances transmit
and receive (both tonally and in reality). The conversation
is funny, engaging, entertaining without being clever.

2003 Advertising

"The voice is consistent and all its own. I can't quite 'see' the person behind Innocent and yet I like them very much. This is a positive. Brands with spokespeople eventually part company with that individual, even if it's Victor Kiam. If I was looking for an embodiment, I'd probably plump for the sadly departed Linda Smith. Innocent has personality that makes surreal jumps of the imagination appear entirely reasoned, if not justified. There's a comedy of the everyday, a fun in the mundane that makes it just so bloody likeable. It's just a packet or bottle of squashed fruit, but it has a life-enhancing brightness to it.

"In my working life, I love the narrative of Innocent. From the off, the founding trio realised the potential for a good story, well told. The really smart part was not letting the notion trickle away in a thousand conversations with their friends and colleagues. They gathered up the ingredients of the story as assiduously as they sourced their mangoes, and turned it into a product. Dan Germain was charged with sending it out into the world. He'd hate it, but he's probably the patron saint of likeableness. I feel selfish, protective, proud and passionate about Innocent. The people who work there are to blame. They could have erred on the side of becoming worthy, repetitive, hectoring, superior or silly. Instead, they have packaged up good fun—or funny goodness—in an effortless way."

Will points out that brands need to think of more channels of communication than before. The advertising business is having to change from its former relatively easy life producing ads for TV, radio or press. As the market became more dynamic, the ad agencies lost control of the relationship with brand owners, and new brand consultancies muscled in. The ad agencies have had to adapt or die, and their clients have had to be alive to this new world order.

"Reaction times have to be swifter, the response to consumer demand and taste decisive and empathetic. Old-fashioned brands that spend all their time thundering from television commercials and do little or no work in packaging and so on are dying on their feet. Innocent has shown that the heavy lifting of marketing communication can be carried out in hand-to-hand combat in the chiller cabinet. In other words, first product, then packaging, lastly advertising. It has been a salutary lesson for the agencies."

Adam Balon is the founder who took charge of commercial activities. He had been marketing manager at Virgin Cola, and before that he had been at McKinsey. He learnt a lot at McKinsey, seeing how business works and how to solve problems. He obviously had a mind that responds to fresh challenges so he joined Virgin to find out more about marketing. It seemed a good move and it was surprisingly hands-on. Virgin is a powerful brand but it operates as a number of smaller businesses. There were only 20 people at Virgin Cola so you could make an impact. Adam loved it for its informal working environment and the absorption in the real world of selling. When it came to carving up Innocent responsibilities between the three of them, his hand went up for "commercial". The reality is that all three are commercial, they all have a flair for marketing, and they all understand the operational needs of the business. There is no sinking of the heart and no lapse of attention when the subject that is not your direct responsibility comes up in a meeting.

Commercial and entrepreneurial are words they are comfortable with. They are proud to be profitable and to see the opportunities that growth creates. And equally happy for people externally to think they are a bunch of students, although I suspect that perception might now have gone for ever. The facts and figures of the business come from their mouths as easily as talk of tasty, little drinks. When I asked for growth figures, the following was given to me in conversation but later confirmed as correct.

Growth Figures: sales (£)

1999	2000	2001	2002	2003	2004	2005	2006	2007
400k	1.6m	4.1m	6.8m	10.7m	17.0m	38.0m	76.0m	115.0m

The figures tell the story that is expressed in words as "the UK's fastest growing food and drink business". They also show a story of regular growth, without any of the blips that even the best companies are prone to. From these sales figures they have made regular profits that they have used to drive further growth – and to help favourite charities, important if they were to create a business to be proud of.

Satisfied customer.

Innocent set out to be Europe's favourite little juice company: a bold ambition lightly expressed. Clearly, they are now well on the way to fulfilling it. In seven years they have gained a 61 per cent share of the UK smoothie market, which is valued at £85m. The reality is that they have virtually created the market because the UK consumer had shown little awareness of smoothies before Innocent's arrival. Now more than 150,000 Innocent smoothies are consumed every day in the UK, and you can buy them in Ireland, Holland, Belgium, France, Alpine (Austria/Switzerland), Germany, Denmark, Sweden and (soon) Norway. They are setting sights towards "the Earth's favourite little food company".

If Innocent gets criticised, it is usually on the grounds of price. "Your stuff's really expensive" is the most common complaint. Price is the crucial commercial decision that any business has to make, and in Innocent's case it was a decision informed by their own knowledge of the market. The founders had an exceptionally clear idea of the typical Innocent consumer: themselves. "People just like us" go to the Jazz on the Green festival, they probably went to university, they enjoy life and spend money on enjoying themselves, they're not as healthy as they'd like to be, they think the world would be better if people were nicer, they work in good jobs in metropolitan areas in the media, consultancy and management. And they can afford to pay £1.80 or more for a 250ml bottle of a juice drink that fits their lifestyle.

As discussed earlier, there are operational reasons why Innocent smoothies are more expensive to make than their competitors'. Innocent keep out the ingredients that other manufacturers use to lower the price. There is a price to pay for 100 per cent natural fruit, no additives, no preservatives, no stabilisers, no concentrates. Innocent decided that their consumers would be prepared to pay that price, particularly when they tasted that the drinks were delicious. Of course, it was tense in the early days when this theory was being tested but the feedback was rapid, particularly because Innocent always made a genuine point of wanting to know what consumers thought. But although the price is relatively high, Maurice Pinto makes the observation that they have always been good at protecting the price and taking costs out. So in real terms Innocent smoothies are now better value than they used to be.

From the point of view of a retailer, there is a distinctive advantage in a premium brand, particularly if that premium brand breaks out of the bounds of being "niche". Innocent has entered the mainstream of consciousness. A big retailer will make more from selling 100 smoothies from Innocent than 100 smoothies from a competitor at half the price. Price is relative, and it needs to be judged against the competition. Innocent have managed to make their brand much more desirable than the competition, making price less of an issue. Innocent is simply better value, if you value your health. The messages to retailers are powerful. Innocent produces a *little guide to selling innocent drinks* in the same format as the *company rule book*. The same format, and the same tone, but with information directed at retailers' concerns: a mixture of hard and soft information. It aims to reassure the retailer that Innocent knows what it is doing, and everything is set out with beguiling simplicity. *National advertising and sampling campaigns, lovely POS and merchandising visits are all there for you, and will definitely drive your volumes.* The message to the retailer is "we care" and we will work with you so that we both sell as much as possible. *Does it work, does it sell?* Your retail customer will want to know. There are figures that make a convincing case, showing:

> Innocent growing by 91 per cent, PJs by ten per cent and own label by 24 per cent. In the same period, other brands declined by 90 per cent. Innocent selling at the rate of 16 units per recipe, per week, per store versus 11 for PJs. The value per week per store being £26 for Innocent and £15 for PJs.

The figures are quoted from AC Nielsen trade research across 192 grocery stores. The overall conclusion, under the heading "What's in it for you?", is this:

> Innocent drinks sell at a higher rate of sale, meaning that you'll make more money. Then there is our commitment to marketing, which far exceeds anyone else's in the sector. Innocent are the most innovative, natural and best tasting drinks out there. We have a burning desire to do everything we can to help your business grow. And we mean everything.

I wanted to know what the relationship was like from the other side of the counter, so I began with two of Innocent's "early adopters" who have stayed with them since. Viktor Hyman is at Barbakan, a bakery and delicatessen that originally served Manchester's Polish community. It has been building its reputation for more than 40 years, and its shop in Chorlton is in a locale for high quality independent food retailers.

> "I'd heard about them and seen their drinks in a vegetarian shop. I recognised that there was something there apart from the freshness, which was important in itself. There's a light-heartedness and an honesty, they've taught me a lot about how to deal with criticism. They've had to deal with jealousy, people resent them

being successful. If they get criticised they leave it
with the person who gives the criticism. They accept
it without anger, in fact with a thank you."

"It seems to me that Innocent is based on truthful
and spiritual principles. They deal like a Buddhist
(I'm not a Buddhist and I don't think they are).
They're ethical but they don't proclaim it. One of
these days, I'm going to make the pilgrimage down
to see them and I'll tell them. But they won't do it,
they won't boast—and they're probably right."

Something unusual is happening here when a retailer,
with no prompting other than the mention of the Innocent
name, starts talking about ethics, pilgrimage and spiritual
principles rather than margins, costs and sales units. It
seems that retailers are not all as hardnosed as the
conventional image. I then spoke to Andrew Sabapathi
of Konditor & Cook near Waterloo in London. Konditor
& Cook make wonderful cakes and they are a growing
brand of the last decade.

"We started off trialling Innocent along with a few other
drinks brands. We liked them a lot and stopped stocking
the other drinks. We liked them for their ethics and simply
because the drinks were the best tasting. But the people
were nice like the drinks, and we sent a cake for a birthday
present. We got invited to Fruitstock and met more of them.
It's not just about juices but people and happiness. But if
you ask them something, they know all the answers.
It's not one of those companies where you ask a question
and they say 'let me find out for you' because there's only
one person who knows. At Innocent everyone knows."

Customers, as well as consumers, can be fans. It might
appear odd, because we are so conditioned to think
otherwise, but good behaviour can also mean good
business. It starts at the level of ordinary conversations

121

The Wall of Acclaim.

that build relationships. In that sense, Innocent's whole approach to selling also reflects its tone of voice. But the relationship with retailers depends both on Innocent remaining absolutely true to itself and on understanding and empathising with the customers' own objectives.

The examples given above are relatively small, independent shops. If Innocent were confined only to that sector, the growth figures quoted earlier would not have been achieved. But Waitrose, Tesco, Sainsbury's and other supermarkets have all embraced Innocent. Mike Luck is the category manager for juices at Sainsbury's.

"I'd first come across Innocent as a customer and they were already in Sainsbury's when I joined in October 2004. They were performing well but the quantities weren't huge. The attraction for Sainsbury's was less to do with volume than associating with a brand that was growing in line with our customer profile. It was a growth opportunity for us and it fitted well with messages like 'Five a day' and Active Kids promotions."

"Innocent are nice people to work with. They go about their business in a friendly way, without the confrontations you sometimes get with bigger brands. They believe in win-win situations, and they're very flexible and open to ideas for exclusive products and special promotions. They're clever people too. They've got great credibility in terms of their numbers, they have the data to support their arguments. I'm sure they'll grow over the next few years, getting into more European countries and new products."

Neil Taylor of The Writer adds another anecdote about Sainsbury's. He was in his local branch doing some shopping and he picked up a carton of Innocent smoothie. Inevitably, he started reading it as the shop assistant rang up the different items he was buying. She said to him, "Read this bit, it's really funny". It's not something that happens with the soap powder or baked beans.

Innocent meets the people.

Trade shows have been important to Innocent. It seems easier for people to understand Innocent when sitting on a bale of hay at a trade show. As well as being good for opening the doors of retailers, they're good for opening the doors to recruits. Lucy Ede, the "Cherry Picker", Number 8, the nutritionist and product developer, met Adam at a trade show when she was working as a food selector for Marks & Spencer. She had seen the drinks and thought them original and funny, then she saw the stand with its bales of hay, trestle tables and chickens. Adam poured her a smoothie and they talked for an hour. Lucy's colleague on the train back remarked "you'll end up working for him". Of course she did. The story shows that Innocent was interested from early on in acquiring real commercial and product expertise.

The people at Innocent are conscious of their relative lack of experience, especially when they look at the competition. Effectively, they are up against Coca-Cola. You cannot buy a Coke smoothie—if you could, you might imagine it would be a little heavy on the sugar—

Lucy Ede.

but if you are thirsty, the choice of drink in a shop might be between a Coke and an Innocent smoothie. Which would you choose and why? Zeinab Malik, an Innocent drinker who works for Sage in Gateshead, wrote the following to me:

> "Innocent labels claim that 'if you're bored' you can call them for a chat—a big difference to the stark 'Freephone Customer Careline 0800 22711' message found on a can of Coca-Cola."

In recent years, there has been a shift in our attitudes. Brands such as Duchy Originals, De Cecco, Konditor & Cook, Dean & Deluca, Green & Black's, Hill Station are quality boutique brands that are spreading more to the mainstream. We are more inclined to trust these brands than the big dinosaurs that have lost some respect. Sometimes, you can point to specific bad news stories that have been damaging—baby food and Nestlé in developing countries, for example. Often, it is simply a reaction against over-processing and a feeling that the brand or product sell-by date has passed. As a result, people are less in awe of Heinz, Coca-Cola, Pepsi than once they might have been.

Innocent certainly respect Pepsi, and it is now the company that they compete most fiercely with. In 2005 Pepsi bought PJs, a UK smoothie brand that had been around a little longer than Innocent. During Innocent's existence, seven or eight new juice companies have started up but failed. PJs was the one that lasted, and its owners sold the company to Pepsi for a tidy sum. Innocent have been expecting a strong assault as a result, but the battle lines are clear. Innocent thinks the competition will keep them on their toes and reinforce their belief in their own product and in the little details

David and Goliath.

that matter to them. Multinationals have rules to adhere to that drive them towards standard products. The belief is that PJs will be less fastidious about its ingredients than Innocent—they have always used concentrates anyway. This makes the product cheaper, a potential advantage in the eyes of the average person on the street. But the difference between the two brands should be obvious. As Richard puts it: "In reality we're being taken on by Pepsi, but there's room for products at the higher and lower end. PJs will be the lower end, and that's fine. We'll be Number 1 through quality, taste, innovation and ethics."

There will be increased competition, possibly from new players who are not yet in the market. Pepsi now have Tropicana smoothies; Nestlé are introducing a new product in 2008. Innocent remains clear and confident about what it is and what it does. Growth is certainly the ambition, but where will it come from? There are three areas that need to be assessed:

Growth by selling more in existing markets
Growth by selling a wider product range
Growth by selling in new markets.

More of the same?

Given that Innocent have a large share of the current UK smoothie market, the first possibility seems the least exciting. But Jon Wright is bullish about the potential.

"In our business plan, we see more and more people wanting healthy juice drinks. People want to get back to quality, simplicity, away from too much processing. What makes the difference? Surely our strawberries aren't that different? What's different is that it's fruit and nothing but fruit. If you have colourings, flavourings, sweeteners, the strawberries don't need any qualities. You only need some strawberries to claim it's a strawberry drink. But the nutritional difference is big. Now we could think of other ideas but actually there's so much we can still do with what we've got, it's a big opportunity."

This does not sound like a company fearing the end of the seam it has been mining. Indeed, the feeling is that the seam is much deeper than anyone imagined at first. The market is still growing by 30 per cent annually. Everything else seems in Innocent's favour too. The growing debate about health, particularly of children, and the increasing consumer suspicion of the big, "over-processed" brands help Innocent. By sticking to what they do, the market should grow quite naturally. They now know what they do inside out, whereas they were certainly feeling their way in the early days. This gives them the confidence to take on even the biggest of competitors. Dan Germain told me:

"It's brilliant that we're up against Pepsi. Look how manoeuvrable we can be. If we decide to do a lychee smoothie, we can put it on the shelves in six weeks. We don't have to go through 60 focus groups, we use our instincts. If we want research, we use the newsletter."

More but different?

There is a tendency among brand experts to want to take a brand and see how far it can stretch into new services and product. It is generally easy to argue the case if it is not your own money at risk.

Innocent have ignored the advice, if it was ever given to them, and have stuck to their smoothies. They have taken the attitude that there is plenty of room for growth if they do that. They have also ignored the ideas that occurred to them for Innocent ice cream, health clubs and nature holidays. Ideas are not in short supply but making them work might create unnecessary distractions.

"We have to keep it focused," says Adam. "It's the best way to be successful. It's about healthy drinks and Europe." This focus, however, does not mean that there are no opportunities for product development. Innovation has always been vital to Innocent, particularly creating new recipes for smoothies. So the simple statement "we stick to smoothies, nothing else" actually conceals the wide range of smoothie varieties that has been produced. Speed of product development and diversity of flavours have been important features of Innocent's success. There have been 35 drink varieties in seven years, and there are 19 different recipes on Innocent drinks on the shelves today (including ingredients such as beetroots, acai berries and figs that you won't find in many other drinks).

Contained in that number are further variants on the mainstream smoothies, in three particular categories. First there are thickies, which contain bio yoghurt, fruit, honey and (sometimes) spices. Thickies have been around since the original smoothies and there is regular product development in this area. The second category is seasonal smoothies. By their nature, these varieties are around for a season, taking advantage of fresh fruit appropriate to spring, summer, autumn and winter. The third category is the super smoothies that are created with a specific purpose in mind. Detox smoothies counter the effects of over-indulgence or simply the modern lifestyle. Vitamin C smoothies are packed with fruit that is rich in Vitamin C for those who might be lacking the vital vitamin. With all these we can see the possibilities for infinite variety, enough to keep tastebuds refreshed if the thought of the same flavour every day starts to become a barrier.

In 2005 it was the right time to launch a new range of products at a completely different market. These are 100 per cent fruit drinks, without the bits you find in the usual smoothies, aimed at children. "Kids are great—smaller, more inquisitive versions of the big lumbering fools that we all grow up to be." The drinks come in a carton that will fit in a child's lunchbox to ensure a healthy element to the school meal. This was the first time that Innocent had really targeted a group outside its perceived core audience of young professionals. It seemed to work, and perhaps it will grow future generations of Innocent drinkers too.

The other significant product development has been Juicy Waters. The idea is simple, explained on the label in the customary Innocent way.

> We had a bit of a to-do here the other day. Jackets off, outside now, in the car park. All because of the juice and water thing. Which is better? Juice or water? The juice camp hold firm in their beliefs—juice has got all of the vitamins to keep you healthy and street tough. But the water people don't give an inch. They counter with talk of rehydration and healthy-looking skin. Who's right? Probably both of them to be honest. Hence this drink. Now pack it in and kiss and make up. That's better.

The bottles are bigger—380ml rather than 250ml for smoothies—which makes for a longer drink. The drink is simply made of fresh fruit, mineral water and natural beet sugar. Concentrates, additives, artificial ingredients are avoided as always. The use of spring water "from the deepest well in Europe" is distinctively Innocent. The modest description is that Juicy Waters are the healthiest version of what they are. When they first started appearing, in 2003, the surprise was that they were available only in Starbucks. Distribution through Starbucks gave Innocent a new level of visibility and also different logistical issues that dictated the nature of the product. There is not the same scope for rapid change between product variants, the production runs are longer, the labels change less frequently.

It was a useful partnership with Starbucks and will have taught Innocent a lot. The relationship in the UK seems to have blossomed because their smoothies also sell in Starbucks now—and Juicy Waters are sold in other outlets so the distribution is not exclusive. The UK relationship even led to some discussion about whether Innocent would work in the USA. The timing wasn't right, but it shows that the thought has been in mind. Perhaps one day the time will be right.

In the meantime, things have moved on with Juicy Waters. Douglas came into Innocent with the brief to find the "Next Big Thing". Before long he decided it was Juicy Waters rather than Nude Holidays for Skiers that would be that Thing; and the product was renamed This Water. This business is now operating separately but under the Innocent wing—with the brief to "beat Innocent". In early 2008 This Water was selling 28 per cent above plan. Perhaps we see here a sign of Innocent's future, as the Board (which includes Doug, new MD of This Water) assesses different brand/business models. Shall we be the Nike of wholefoods? Or the Unilever of drinks?

Wider still and wider?

The USA would have been an opportunistic development, rather than one in Innocent's plan to be the favourite

The French office.

juice company in Europe by 2010. The plans for growth in Europe are developing, with operations opening first in Ireland, then Benelux, followed by France, Germany, Alpine countries and most of Scandinavia. The focus remains on healthy drinks and Europe. But what about cultural differences, particularly when language has been such a distinctive part of the Innocent brand?

The approach has been gradualist. Dublin is the most established of the Innocent overseas offices (Dub Towers). Language was not an issue in Ireland but the use of the Irish office number is recent. The operation runs like a small, but Irish, version of the parent, and the Innocent TV ad has run with an Irish voiceover. In Benelux, small versions of the company rule book were used in translation around the neck of the bottle; the ingredients were listed in Dutch and French, but the main label narrative is in English. This will change soon when Innocent start selling their large cartons throughout the Netherlands. France is in its very early days. It has the reputation of being a difficult market to crack for a non-native brand. But *Le Monde* has written about Innocent: "Chez Innocent, on interpelle le client avec des etiquettes humoristiques sur les bouteilles." So at least the French know about the funny labels.

Adam is leading the European development, so I asked him about the difficulties (or not).

"Recruiting is difficult. And there are cultural differences. The same brand of humour might not work in Paris.
You get around that by finding great people and trusting them—'they get it'. They have to understand the cultural aspects of our business, what Innocent is all about, and they have to know how things are done in that country."

"So you have to rely on the same things that work in the UK, and of course we still make the smoothies here.

Paris is as close as Manchester so transport's not an issue. In France, we need to fast-track word of mouth recommendations, do talks in business schools, meet style leaders. The consumers we want would want to work with us. But we need to find the best ways of reaching them. We think the Innocent proposition is a relatively multinational one. There are the same consumer trends, people looking for drinks that are healthy and that taste good, and a business that's ethical. To be credible you have to stand for the same fundamental principles everywhere. If you really believe in what you do, the selling is simple."

Adam tells me, in that musing Innocent way, that they have been thinking about running a business plan competition in Scandinavia. Want to run Innocent Denmark? *Send us your business plan.* It's a thought. Perhaps no other business would seriously entertain such a thought but with Innocent you think it might just work. It might just achieve that fusion of the altruistic and the commercial that is distinctively Innocent.

A hiccup

One disadvantage of getting bigger is that people start seeing you in a different light. They start watching for mistakes to be made. To many people it seemed that Innocent had made a big mistake when, in Spring 2007, it was announced that McDonald's would be selling Innocent kids' smoothies in its Happy Meals. It would be a pilot scheme in one region of England, the north-east, and would last six months.

"It's all about money and you won't be getting any more of mine," wrote one blogger on the Innocent website. That kind of comment seemed typical at first: many Innocent drinkers reacted as if the company had just sold its business to the US corporation. People assumed that McDonald's was after an Innocent halo effect. No one imagined that association with McDonald's would add any lustre to the Innocent brand—only sales volume.

That seemed to work Innocent fans into a state of animation that ranged from disbelief to disgust to anger. If membership cards existed for Innocent they would have been torn up or burnt. The company's blog could hardly contain the torrent of words.

Some of the words were supportive but most were along the lines of "wish you hadn't". By the end of the first day Richard Reed had to go on the blog to put out a conciliatory statement. After all this was a company that had grown at an astonishing rate because its customers felt part of a close, like-minded family. The statement went along the lines of "surely it's better for children to get the chance to drink healthy fruit smoothies than the kind of stuff more usually available from McDonald's."

For many of the bloggers this seemed a red rag rather than a reasoned argument. "It's not about kids it's about ethics," thundered the ironically-named Mac. Some would never be reconciled to "McDollar"—they shouldn't be touched with a banana.

When I spoke to Richard soon after the storm broke he was battered but unrepentant.

> "Obviously, we expected to get a kicking from some of our drinkers for going into McDonald's but when a company slated for selling unhealthy food asks to start selling healthy food, it felt more irresponsible to say no than yes. And our strategy has always been to do what we think is right not what we think sounds right. And we weren't going to change from that philosophy now, even though we knew we would get some flak."

Despite outward appearances, Innocent Drinks is not a hippy commune. They know that they're in business to make money, and without profits they'll never be able to do the good things they want to do. But McDonald's is a no-go area for many people, even if organisations like Greenpeace are finding ways to work with them without abandoning ethics. And Greenpeace's approval was an important element in Innocent's decision to go ahead.

Aware of the sensitivity Innocent had got all its staff together twice to debate the decision. They knew that it would be controversial inside the business. This was quite a baptism of fire for Jamie Mitchell, Innocent's relatively new UK managing director. But he emerged positive about the debate that had been generated.

> "The blog was extraordinary—not just the scale of it but the quality of the debate. We're saddened if we lose even one Innocent drinker as a result of this. But we surprised thirty or more of them by ringing them up for a conversation—suddenly an Innocent founder was on the line. We might not have convinced them but at least we've reached a point where we know we respect each other's position."

Jamie Mitchell admits Innocent's naivety in not realising quite how negative the reaction would be. Innocent had sounded out Greenpeace and the Rainforest Alliance, both of whom were working with McDonald's to combat rainforest destruction. The decision came down to ethics and health, and on both counts Innocent decided that the best policy was to go ahead with the trial.

> "How could we stand aside if McDonald's want to sell healthier food to children? Our objective is to get kids to have more fruit. We couldn't just stand

outside being angry. We want our drinks to reach kids wherever they are—that means schools and family restaurants. So we're aiming for both of those."

Ian Hindle, a McDonald's spokesman, put it to me like this:

"Our customers are the ultimate decision-makers. It will be up to them whether they choose Coke, Tropicana, water or an Innocent smoothie. But we want to offer them the healthier option."

So was this all a terrible mistake? A year later the furore has died down. The McDonald's trial continues, this time in a different region. Innocent people are still defiant but not willing to extend the trial to include adult smoothies. Everyone is still keen to get across the main health message. And Dan is proud of the way Innocent talked to its drinkers throughout the debate.

"Personally I think the greatest thing is that we've been able to have a proper, open debate on our blog. I'm proud that that's the way we do things at Innocent. No smoke, no mirrors."

The evidence from Innocent drinkers is that only 9 per cent thought it was a bad idea to sell Innocent kids' smoothies in McDonald's. There was a lot of negative publicity, from those seeking to knock, but a lot more positive publicity about the way Innocent had coped.

When we're older, sitting in our retirement cottage, smoking a pipe whilst wistfully gazing out to sea, we quite fancy being proud of the stuff we did when we were younger. That's why we started the innocent foundation, a separate registered charity. Part of the profit from the sale of these smoothies is given to the charity, meaning that just by drinking these drinks you're helping people in the countries where our fruit is grown and where our drinks are sold. Find out a bit more at www.innocentfoundation.org

An innocent promise
We promise that anything innocent will always taste good and do you good. We promise that we'll never use concentrates, preservatives, stabilisers, or any weird stuff in our drinks. And if we do you can tell our mums.

Label, 2006.

Chapter Six

Be Responsible

My grandfather said:
"Do good business and the money will take care
of itself."

Maurice Pinto

Responsibility sounds like a challenging issue for any brand, compared to the more blatantly businesslike requirements to be commercial or entrepreneurial. Yet surely every brand needs to be responsible, even if prompted only by the increasingly prevalent corporate and social responsibility report. But who do you need to be responsible to? Innocent interprets its responsibilities much more widely than many other brands, and perhaps it is this that sets it apart from others.

Responsibility starts with the product itself. Innocent produce drinks that taste good and are good for you. It is unusual to have the opportunity to do something to improve your health that is also enjoyable and completely without a downside. Running is good for you too—but you don't necessarily enjoy it when you feel that stitch in your side. You can indulge your taste in smoothies secure in the thought that, perhaps unusually, even excess will leave hardly any after-effects. There are very few products like that. If the company you work for makes bombs or cigarettes, is your conscience completely clear? If you sell shoes or let shops, if you balance the books or design the books, if you deliver goods or make good deals, can you say that what you do never has a bad effect?

This idea of naturally doing good through the product you make has an influence on the whole philosophy of the company and the brand. Unlike many other companies that might claim to be "responsible" Innocent can approach the subject with the absolute minimum of guilt. It is not a case of being responsible because you know you have a questionable effect on individuals, society or the planet—of having to produce a PR campaign to head off inevitable criticism. The irony is, of course, that there might be more rumblings of

141

conscience in Fruit Towers than in the munitions factory, but that is simply the people they are. Without being smug they recognise responsibilities and they wish to live up to them.

The "be responsible" brand value is the most moralistic of the Innocent values. *Be true to our principles, and do what we believe is right. To be conscious of the consequences of our actions, in both the short and long term. To leave things a little better than we find them, and to encourage others to join us too.*

Religious comparisons seem unavoidable but they are also unfair because Innocent wears its belief too lightly to be thought of as religious in any fundamental sense. Although there are strongly held beliefs, there is never an attempt to preach or to hector people into sharing those beliefs. If this is religion it is a thoroughly modern kind, the kind we have yet to experience in any existing church, temple or holy house. There is simply too much laughter and good humour involved.

The articles of faith for Innocent were expressed in a recent advert with the headline, "Hello. Here are six nice reasons to drink our smoothies." Then with six arrows pointing at the smoothie carton, the reasons were listed as:

- our smoothies are made with fresh juices rather than concentrates
- over 100% RDA of natural vitamin C in every 250ml glassful
- each carton contains at least 8 portions of fruit
- they all have a low GI score—more fibre than a bowl of bran flakes in each 250 ml serving
- tests have shown they make you more attractive to the opposite sex*

*our same sex variant should be hitting the shelves in early 2007

In the kitchen.

Innocent believes that its prime responsibility is to the health of its consumers. It understands the art of persuasion so it avoids the preachy approach implied by the descriptions in its "be responsible" value. It knows that a spoonful of sugar (as long as it's natural beet) helps the medicine go down; the sixth reason, after the five short sharp jabs of facts, is an Innocent joke. But even the joke is trying to be nice to everyone in a responsible way. There are several layers of playfulness, but the core message is serious.

The belief is that Innocent drinks are as natural as they can make them. By avoiding chemicals and additives they make life more difficult for themselves but more healthy for their consumers. The one kind of processing that can be said to stray from the wholly natural is flash pasteurisation, but this derives from a recognition that there would be an unacceptable health concern without it. Cases of infants in the USA being killed by unpasteurised fruit juices cause Innocent to err on the side of safety. The people at Innocent believe that pasteurisation—a process of heating the juice, then cooling it, to reduce harmful bacteria—is necessary. They also believe that flash pasteurisation has no effect on taste or on the nutritional profile of their juices. Recognising the value of freshness, the sell-by (or "enjoy-by") dates are relatively short.

Responsibility for making sure Innocent drinks are as healthy and fresh as possible is the everyday concern of Lucy Ede and her team of nutritionists and product developers. You can recognise them in Fruit Towers by their white coats and you can generally spot them at work tasting new recipes through the glass walls of the kitchen lab. It sounds like a tough job, and it probably is, but we can all recognise certain compensations.

Lucy tasting ingredients.

This is a revelation, not particularly deep, that came from meeting Lucy and her team for a tasting.

It comes down to this. The basic philosophy of Innocent is that food can be lifesaving stuff, so they want to make as much of the food that saves lives as possible. To be innocent not guilty. They do not want to take any responsibility for producing food that has any bad effect on health, but they are very happy to be responsible for producing more of the good kind—and persuading more of us to have more of it. But, as they also say, a lot of healthy stuff tastes rubbish. "Man cannot live on mung beans alone." Eat more fruit and veg. Eat more natural produce. Let us help by making it taste good. Lucy Ede explains more:

> "When you're developing new drinks you can't stray from the strategy—it's simple and natural, drinks that taste good

145

and do good naturally. We can't add anything, we have
to use nature to do the job. So we have to find ways, for
example, to combine carrots with fruit and keep the drink
stable—and to be consistent all year round. That means
knowing all about the qualities and varieties of fruit."

In the early days, it was difficult to persuade suppliers
and manufacturing partners of the rightness of their
cause. A big enough body of consumers was already
convinced, so Innocent were able to point to their success
with this group to bring people on side. Innocent had
no track record, no established brand at that time. It
took hard work, persistence and skills of persuasion to
convince suppliers of the merits of being 100 per cent
natural. But it happened, and the relationships established
in those early days still continue. Innocent is the biggest
buyer of Indian Alphonso mangoes in Europe, thanks to
the success of the mangoes and passion fruits smoothie.
Alphonso mangoes are more expensive than other
varieties but Innocent uses 100 per cent Alphonsos in
its drinks, resisting the temptation to blend them with
cheaper, less tasty varieties. The challenge has been to
source another supplier, not to replace the original but
to provide back-up in case the crop fails. Commitment
to suppliers, shown over a long term, helps persuade
new partners to change the way they produce essentials
to meet Innocent's demands.

"We're not driven by cost but by quality. We believe
our consumers are prepared to pay the price not just for
health and taste but for ethics. It means we have better
long-term relationships with our suppliers and we build
partnerships. That helps us too with our remit to produce
more recipes faster than anyone. We aim to be the first
to market with unusual fruits, which often have a specific
health benefit, such as pomegranates. We certainly turn
projects around faster than anyone else in the industry."

The responsibility to consumers leads naturally to broader responsibilities to the communities where Innocent suppliers are based, and to the planet itself. Richard Reed talks about the wish to become the first FMSG (Fast Moving *Sustainable* Good) company to differentiate Innocent's approach from some of its less environmentally and ethically sensitive competitors in the FMCG sector. But he realises too that this responsibility, and the reputation for being ethically sound, brings with it rather scary needs—particularly the need to be good, not just to be seen to be good.

Richard and some Rainforest Alliance certified bananas, Costa Rica, 2006.

Innocent now has its own sustainability squad that looks at four areas:

- products
- Innocent's own "corporate behaviour"
- packaging
- emissions

Richard makes this area of the business his personal responsibility. It starts with the products, where Lucy is his ally in making sure that things are natural and healthy. But it then goes further, into the way ingredients are sourced for smoothies and what happens in the countries and on the farms where Innocent buys its raw materials.

> "We've no need to pretend, but we know we're not yet good enough. We're just starting. Success and principles can strengthen each other. You can profit from being decent. We want to change the system so that other businesses can see you can make money from being good. We're a £38m company giving half a million back. We set up the Innocent Foundation to give us the best way to do it. It's easy to get the image but we want to get the reality. Our communications must represent what we are rather than try to dress us up as better than we are."

Innocent accepts that it has to operate as a role model, which means not criticising others. Although it has a deep interest in environmental issues, it strives not to make "environment" the message. It's a smoothie company, and everything else follows from that. It makes choices all the time with its products and behaviour, but these remain focused on the need to create the best and most natural drinks. Other companies use ascorbic acid to stop fruit going brown; Innocent uses Sicilian lemon juice. This does the job, it costs a bit more money, but it's natural.

A question has been nagging at Innocent: who measures the measurers? If Innocent decides that eight passion fruits and two bananas go into a smoothie, how do they know that those ingredients are as pure and natural as they want them to be? Obviously, they have their own expertise now and there is no need to take everything on trust. Relationships have been forged and strengthened over the years with suppliers. Visits to the farms is a good safeguard. But the nagging question remained until Innocent entered a formal agreement with the Rainforest Alliance.

By working with the Rainforest Alliance, Innocent reassures itself (and others) that its products and suppliers reach agreed standards. This stringent system, involving audits and accreditation by an independent, non-commercial expert organisation, is built on top of the practice that had evolved over the previous seven years. The steps in the system include suppliers needing to comply with ILO (International Labour Organisation) standards even to get to the table; then taking part in an assessment of environmental and social practices. A visit from the Innocent ingredients team follows. Now the involvement of the Rainforest Alliance adds a further degree of stringency to the process. The relationship with the Rainforest Alliance has been further strengthened by Innocent's funding worth $30,000 a year. This gives Innocent a man on the ground, Carlos based in Central America. With Carlos' help, Innocent has found new and certificated farms for bananas and pineapples.

In May 2006, the Innocent newsletter featured Richard's visit to a supplier in Costa Rica, in the foothills of the Orosi volcano where a lot of Innocent's fruit is grown. There he met the president and other officials from the Rainforest Alliance, as well as growers. The message got as serious as Innocent ever allows itself to be in its external communications.

> "In case you didn't know, the Rainforest Alliance is an independent, non-commercial entity that audits farms and fruit plantations in a holistic fashion. It looks at things as a whole, employing natural techniques to replace agrochemicals, ensuring price and wage premiums and better social conditions for workers, and perhaps most importantly, making sure that all of this helps to protect the biodiversity of the land where we grow our fruit."

The Rainforest Alliance in action, educating in Costa Rica, 2006.

The outcome of the trip is that all Innocent bananas are now bought from Rainforest Alliance sources. There is the serious message but, as ever with Innocent, it is treated in a light way. It's always possible to see a funnier side, particularly when you have a photograph of Richard in a shed full of rotting banana skins that are being composted into fertiliser. Add a few stories about pig feed, flies and parasitic wasps, and any envy of Richard's situation disappears in a low rumble of chuckles.

A 100 per cent recycled plastic bottle.

But sustainability can begin at home. After taking all this trouble to make sure the fruit in the bottle is natural, what about the bottle itself? Early in Innocent's history, the company started using plastic bottles made from 25 per cent recycled material. This was a high proportion at the time, and improved when the proportion went up to 50 per cent in 2005. The search for improvement continued, and in 2007 Innocent introduced the world's first 100 per cent recycled plastic bottle.

One of the new people to come into Innocent over the last couple of years is Jess Sansom. Jess is full of that positive Australian spirit and regarded with some awe by the founders. She has a degree in environmental science, and a masters degree in environmental law. She moved from consultancy to McDonald's where she worked in the US and Europe in very corporate surroundings, aiming to push up environmental standards. With some success, it has to be said, as McDonald's is no longer regarded as quite the demon it once was. The move to Innocent came in February 2007.

"Rich, Adam and Jon wanted to take sustainability
further. I was attracted by that. They were thinking about
the next phase of sustainability, and I thought I could
do that at a smaller, flexible company like Innocent."

The Innocent approach to these issues in 2008 is noticeably more sophisticated than when I carried out my original research two years earlier. Now Jess is managing a three-pronged programme, finding ways to improve:

- sourcing of ingredients
- packaging
- resource efficiency.

DGV (Dancing Grass Van).

The appointment of Carlos ("with a great moustache") from the Rainforest Alliance is one big step forward. He is effectively funded by a $30,000 donation that Innocent makes annually to the Rainforest Alliance. But Jess sees this initiative as just a beginning. After all, the Rainforest Alliance covers only some of the countries where Innocent sources fruit. She's bringing in statements of minimum standards and best practice that all suppliers will be bound by, insisting that it will be done in a way that is not a burden to the farmers. There is also a programme of visiting suppliers to get closer to them,

153

so that Innocent can better understand quality and sustainability issues.

There have been big advances in Innocent's packaging materials. The smoothie bottles are now 100 per cent recycled (and the thickies will follow), and the labels are made from 25 per cent recycled paper with 75 per cent from Forest Stewardship Council certified trees. In fact this paper is specially made for Innocent. Given the hostile environment in a packing factory, with the susceptibility of recycled paper to tearing, 25 per cent is a high proportion.

Perhaps the most ambitious programme started as work to reduce carbon footprints but has now broadened to resource efficiency. Three carbon audits have been carried out, looking at the footprint from the farm through every link of the supply chain. The move to recycled plastic has brought big reductions. Each Innocent team is being trained in environmental awareness, but Jess is not content to focus on Innocent's own use of resources. She is talking seriously with all the suppliers, persuading them "with a little encouragement" towards more action on energy, waste and water. She's proud of the suppliers who started a waste project and saved 54 per cent in six months. The company then decided, in the style of Innocent, to donate 10 per cent of the ongoing savings made to charity.

The next big challenge for Innocent will be water footprinting. Jess reels off scary figures about water usage in different industries. But although she uses such figures to prick your conscience, she sees her role as a commercial one. The facts show that Innocent's approach to sustainability issues is now reducing costs and saving money. And the higher the price of oil, the more the overall costs move in Innocent's favour.

With all this as background, it seems logical for Innocent to decide to share some of the wealth they create with people who need it more. Each year, 10 per cent of profits gets paid into the Innocent Foundation, a separate registered charity. The foundation is run by Linda, who brings a career-long experience of working with Oxfam and NGOs. Innocent is proud to use 10 per cent for what it sees as good causes, but equally proud to use the 90 per cent to grow its own business. Innocent's continuing growth, and increasing profits, will fund the foundation.

The Innocent Foundation was set up in July 2004. It was designed to bring cohesion and strategy to a whole series of good works and good causes that Innocent had supported since its founding days. These ranged from tree planting in UK cities to giving smoothies to the homeless, as well as developing projects in the countries where Innocent sources its fruit. The foundation now works in partnership with community based projects and NGOs in the countries that supply the largest amount of Innocent's fruit and have the greatest need (identified by the UN Development Need Index). These countries are India, Colombia, Ecuador and Costa Rica in 2006. But the foundation also supports projects in countries with real need, even if Innocent does not currently buy fruit from those countries. African countries benefit, and also particular causes such as post-tsunami regeneration.

The range of projects supported is enormous. Iracambi aims to protect Brazil's Amazon rainforest by making its conservation more attractive to the local community than its destruction. Send a Cow is about enabling rural African communities to run small farms sustainably. Find Your Feet helps women in rural Indian communities to improve access to water and promote sustainable farming. Groundwork regenerates deprived areas of the UK, helping a West London school with replanting. Chicks (Country Holidays for Inner City Kids) helps children to go on holiday in the countryside.

Chicks was the chosen charity of the Fruitstock Festival, which Innocent ran every summer from 2003 to 2006. The other name originally considered, Glastonberry, gives you an idea of what Fruitstock is like: a music festival in a field over a weekend in summer. It doesn't have the hype or the big names of Glastonbury itself—and, thanks to luck with the weather, there has been an absence of mud.

The field in question also happens to be in Regent's Park, London, so this is a metropolitan event rather than an attempt at a country idyll. Rural life does come to Fruitstock, in the form of the farmer's market.

The idea of Fruitstock goes back to pre-Innocent days. The obvious inspiration is the Jazz on the Green festival where Innocent launched itself and received a full "yes" bin of empty bottles. Fruitstock is a bigger and better recreation of the Parsons Green event, set in Regent's Park because the Royal Parks wanted to encourage more popular use of the parks. Yet Richard's sister sets it back a little further in evolutionary history: "He's just trying to recreate Upper Hopton Gala." We all have our roots: some people use them better than others.

There are other streams feeding into Fruitstock. When Jessica (Number 17) joined Adam's sales team in February 2002 she ran sampling campaigns and road shows. At that time too there used to be a birthday party for Innocent people, friends and journalists. The party simply got bigger and bigger and by 2003 became an event that needed proper planning to avoid any prospect of public humiliation. There was a real fear that the festival might flop. Jessica explains: "We said it was free. But would anyone come? We had no idea what to expect."

It was an unfortunate twist that on the Friday, the day before Fruitstock started, Jessica went down with food poisoning. She rang in distraught and spoke to Adam. He asked for instructions and was pointed towards Jessica's pink book on her desk. This set out what needed to be done: a lot. Adam, Jon and Richard got everyone to stop work, gathered them together and made sure that Fruitstock happened. It was a moment when everyone came together and joined in. Dan S made his chutney, others made muffins, others collected parasols. Innocent people converged on the park where contractors and partners were assembling tents, stalls and stands. When they all came back on Saturday, 39,000 people also arrived. News had spread by word of mouth, email, flyers around the parks, a little advertising and listings in guides. Nothing big had been intended, simply a relaxed celebration with healthy food and drinks and live music. When people got back to work after the weekend, Innocent were inundated with emails from people saying how much they had loved Fruitstock. So the determination set in to do it another year, but to make it bigger, better and more Innocent.

Fruitstock grew year by year, with a steady improvement in the quality of the music and in numbers of people attending. Planning for things not to go right included the printing of waterproof ponchos with the message "at least it's not snowing".

These were not needed. The sun has always shone on Fruitstock and in 2005 100,000 people turned up to hear an eclectic mix of music including Nitin Sawhney, the London Community Gospel Choir, Nate James and the Innocent Drum Club. As well as the music, there were tents and marquees all around the perimeter, as if gathered for a medieval joust. In the tents you could meet people (there was even a "flirting area"), and you could buy all sorts of good food and drink. The Farmer's Market was billed as the UK's biggest, with UK standing for Uncle Ken (if you wanted to know). The usual festival add-ons—face painting for kids, first aid and merchandise could be found around the stages and the stalls. And at the end of it all Innocent could still agree with what it had said in advance: "We still strive to make the best-tasting drinks in the world and we still like to spend weekends in the park dancing badly." Along the way £100,000 was raised for charity.

Innocent was keen to try to make the festival better but not necessarily bigger. There was some concern that the music was becoming too dominant, so new stalls and activities were added, among them the Penguin Classics outdoor "library"—bookshelves full of the best books ever written for people to borrow and relax in a Penguin deckchair while they read. People could drink coffee served from Penguin Classics mugs—or of course drink an Innocent smoothie. Penguin staff could recommend books and authors, and also invite people to join in the weekend-long poll to find out Fruitstock's favourite classic. For the children there was the chance to meet and listen to authors and storytellers in the Puffin Reading Area.

You can tell a brand by the company it keeps. Brand partnerships send messages about each of the brands involved, and here Innocent and Penguin are happy to be seen in each other's company, one to provide healthy food for the body, the other healthy food for the mind. Penguin is a brand that has been around for more than 70 years, establishing a place of trust and affection in the minds of the book-reading public, but keen to have a little of Innocent's younger, funnier brand character rub off on its marketing. This was a relationship that seemed to fit well and a thought that would feed into Innocent's contemplation about the future direction of Fruitstock.

Fruitstock's success came at a price. It absorbed about half a million pounds of money but that was not the reason for rethinking it. Fruitstock had become a music festival in its own right and Innocent decided that it didn't want to be a music company. Innocent, in Dan's

Fruitstock 2005.

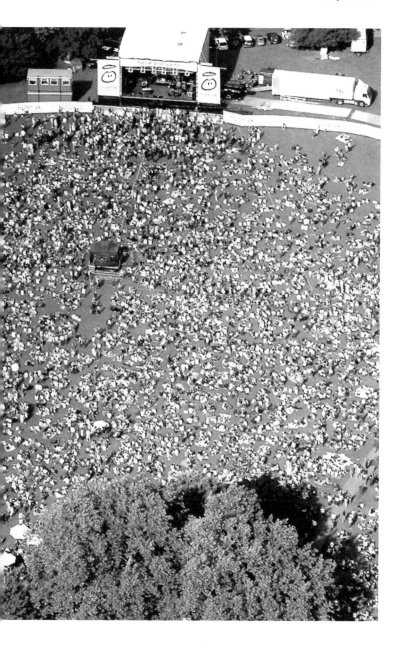

words, is "about fruit, nature and being decent to each other". With the crowds at Fruitstock it became difficult to move around and relax, and there were health and safety issues, particularly as the venue was one of the Royal Parks. So the thought became: what would our ideal summer party be like? The answer came back, like a Village Fete. This would be smaller in scale, less about music, better for younger children and families, and more fun for Innocent people because of a range of daft activities that you would find in village fetes up and down the country. The difference was that you might not expect welly wanging, ferret racing and Morris dancing to be on offer at a village fete in the centre of London.

The decision was taken to hold the Village Fete in Regent's Park but to limit numbers to 60,000—half the number of the last Fruitstock. The limit would be applied by making it a ticketed event (£5 entrance) and giving the money raised to charity. Ailana saw it like this:

> "It felt calmer, more family-oriented. There was more sitting around, enjoying life at a slower pace. There were lovely things to do. You could try duck herding."

All in all, it felt more Innocent, more responsible: "to leave things a little better than we find them, and to encourage others to join us too".

Fruitstock 2006.

Village Fete, 2007.

Chapter Seven

The Future's Fruit

The attraction of Innocent was the single-minded view of the brand.

Charlotte Rawlins

It's the end of April 2008. Innocent is nine years old and holding its first AGM. For Innocent that means A Grown-up Meeting. As I walk up to the door of Fruit Towers I'm greeted by a succession of smiling Innocent people. It's a bit like school open day. In no time at all Claire, Kay and Hannah have separately introduced themselves to me and asked if I would like a smoothie.

The AGM fills the Innocent offices with more than a hundred customers whose names have been pulled out of a ballot. Over a thousand people applied to give up their Saturday afternoons to go along to the AGM. Other companies have AGMs for shareholders and, except for times of crisis, wonder if anyone will turn up.

The formal bit of the afternoon consists of Jon, Richard and Adam giving us talks about Innocent's progress over the last year. Richard says that the company's purpose is to "make food good" and the audience nods reassurance to him and themselves. This is what they believe Innocent should be for. A simple word like "good" in Innocent mouths has a meaning that applies to quality, health and sustainability. He explains how they took account of the Science Advisory Committee to decide what food might be Innocent or otherwise: fruit, vegetables, wholegrains and dairy qualify. The fifth healthy ingredient–oily fish–is not really smoothies material.

So there is now a business litany that moves from using **healthy products** (100 per cent natural) to **ethically grown** produce to **sustainable packaging** to **resource efficiency** and then to **sharing the proceeds**. There is a pride in leaving a positive legacy for the future and the ambition becomes bigger year by year. From West London's favourite little juice company to London's, England's, the UK's, Europe's before reaching, in time, the Earth's favourite little food company.

Along the way, reviewing the last year, there have been highs and lows. The highs include more and more recipes, a steady expansion through Europe and the move to 100 per cent recycled plastic bottles. Competition is growing from the big corporations like Pepsico (Tropicana) and Nestlé (Boost) but the big boys are finding Innocent difficult to bully. Adam reports that Pepsico had challenged Innocent's claim that "smoothies are better for you than juice". The complaint went to the Advertising Standards Authority (ASA) and was not upheld. Smoothies are better than juices.

The year's lows contain lessons. A bad batch of strawberries fermented, making a lot of smoothies gaseous and fizzy. The batch was recalled. The need to keep a close watch at all time, even during Christmas and New Year, was emphasised. The McDonald's furore was both high and low. In the end the Innocent founders seem upbeat about selling healthy drinks to McDonald's customers. It seems better than McDonald's customers not having the choice; and nearly all the audience, on a show of hands, agrees.

After this the afternoon becomes lighter. Next there are small groups gathered in different parts of Fruit Towers. The groups are led by Innocent staff to discuss ideas for packaging, design, words for labels and many other topics. Ideas are contributed freely and in great profusion by customers. This beats commissioning McKinsey, and it seems that Innocent has found its own way of gaining management consultancy advice from customers. Tea and cakes mix easily with questions and answers. It works only because those customers believe in the cause. It has the feel of a particularly benign political movement. A political movement with no trace of cynicism, and built on two-way trust.

It used to be a truism that brands depend on trust. Of course, brands need you and me to trust them because otherwise we would not buy whatever it is they are selling. Sometimes this gets changed into: "our brand is built on trust". Or even: "our brand values include trust". All of this is rather dubious because the decision, whether to trust or not, does not rest with the brand—it rests with the consumer of the brand.

In the case of Innocent, consumers decided that they would trust the brand. They decided this despite Innocent playing with their thought processes even as they pondered the question of trust. There in the ingredients, for example, after the real fruit ingredients, it says "a few small pebbles"—and, lower down, "we lied about the pebbles". How did a brand that deliberately lies, and cheerfully admits to lying, come to be regarded as an upholder of ethics and standards? The times are out of joint. We have become so used to not believing anything that we believe only what we are told not to believe at all.

Certainly we reserve judgement on most brands, never wholeheartedly believing that they will always tell the truth. Brands have become a bit like politicians; the only sensible attitude is to mistrust them. The more brands "spin" the less inclined we are to believe them. You might regard this book as an example of brand spin. It includes more than a few small lies. But I lied about the lies.

I asked Sarah McCartney of Lush what she thought were Innocent's strengths as a brand. She replied: "I'd be hard pressed to choose between Innocent's two powers: really tasty products and telling the truth. With my arm twisted behind my back, I've got to say that it's the consistent quality of the products that wins out.

Without that, any brand is meaningless." As Sarah knows better than anyone, a brand cannot communicate without using words. So we have to give as much care as we can to a brand's words. But we have to be aware that words will always be open to question. All you can really trust is what's left once you've stripped away all the words, all the tools of communication: the product itself, fruit and nothing but nothing but fruit.

Except...

We do not have to choose between the purity of the product and the purity of the brand. To a remarkable extent, in the case of Innocent, the two are so closely linked as to be inseparable.

We cannot strip away the words that make up the brand any more than we could strip away the fruit and still have a smoothie. Innocent is of one piece; it has a consistency in every encounter, at every place where you come into contact with it. There is an absence of side, a lack of pomposity, an avoidance of nastiness. Perhaps it is hard to sink into a stream of conventionally competitive managerialese when you are sunk into a beanbag in an open-plan office with Astroturf under your feet.

Being nice to people is Innocent's gift to a cynical world. Business leaders will try to convince you that the way to the top is by being selfishly decisive and ruthlessly focused. Innocent shows that there is another way, and perhaps this other way works better. It involves being sensitive, considerate and aware of wider responsibilities to everyone whose lives you touch in any small way. And it means being all those things while displaying a natural sense of humour that disarms criticism.

169

I suspect that there are dissertations and theses coming out of business schools that demonstrate the perils of humour. Like fine wine, it does not travel. Like an avocado it's a matter of personal taste. Like a banana, it does not last. Like a smoothie, humour is not a complete meal in itself. But, like a smoothie, it makes life more enjoyable, more worth living, and it does you good. We can all do with more of it. Perhaps there are times and places when you need something else, a double espresso or a kir royale, a stern prohibition or a moment of meditation. But humour can fit more smoothly into different business situations than we often give it permission to do. Innocent shows that you can try humour and that it generally works if it is always aware of the need for truth.

When taking inspiration from Innocent, other brands need to take care not to misinterpret Innocent's light touch, based on honesty and respect, for a crude dig in the ribs. The Innocent brand is based on its own clear understanding of its values. Humour is simply one means of demonstrating its own distinctive approach to those values. As with any brand, you can state a value—entrepreneurial, for example—but such a word can be interpreted in any number of ways by any number of people. Words are slippery things, they slip out of your mouth and out of your mind in strange ways. And they enter another person's mind in a different disguise. Innocent's success has been in sharing its understanding of its brand values first with the inner core of its founding management, then with its employees, suppliers, customers and consumers. There is a high degree of unity about what the brand stands for. There is also remarkably little dissonance between what Innocent believes it is about and what its audiences perceive it

The Big Knit project. Visit www.innocentdrinks.co.uk/thebigknit

to be about. Other brands, and bigger brands, envy this. There is some envy of Innocent that could turn into a backlash if enough people decided that, this year, being good is bad. We live in fashion-conscious times. The fashion that dictates Innocent's current desirability might turn in time. Yet there remains the core of Innocent's brand values that protects it from the worst that cynicism or antagonism can throw at it. Humour is disarming, so too are genuine good works, a naturally healthy product and a commitment to be generous. "Do no evil" is the proclamation by the Google brand but it's a saying that associates itself more convincingly with Innocent.

The communications of many brands revolve entirely around content. Innocent understands that, vital as the message is, the way you deliver the message makes all the difference. Innocent takes its lead for the delivery from its own consumers. Innocent people are generally writing for their friends and, often, for their mums. I suspect most business writing would improve if people wrote for their mothers.

There is a strong sense of family in Innocent. People join Innocent and they join a family. They also find themselves joining their own family to Innocent. Despite talk of the modern family being dysfunctional, it remains the most cohesive social unit we have. It connects us with our past, present and future. As long as its family sense remains strong, Innocent's future will be assured.

In the end it comes down to two things that bind the family together: the brand and the fruit. The two are inseparably connected, like the ingredients in a perfectly blended smoothie, and people will continue to buy Innocent because they love both the brand and the fruit. The brand is about being natural, staying healthy and enjoying life, with drinks made of fresh fruit as the means to help you achieve those aims. The result is the absolute simplicity of Innocent, a brand made of fruit and nothing but fruit.

Seven pillars of innocent wisdom...

1. keep it natural
2. stay focused on the brand
3. your business is an extended family
4. use your brain and your imagination
5. stick to your principles
6. think about the mess you leave behind you
7. enjoy yourself

Innocent, 2010.

Afterword

Skip forward to Spring 2011. Spring is surely Innocent's season. There is something about Spring – a sense of optimism, natural growth, increasing brightness – that fits the Innocent personality better than dreary winter.

So I'm sitting with Richard Reed in a little room in Fruit Towers. Sunshine streams through the windows, there's the growth of a beard on Richard's face, and a sign on the wall that says "Room booking – Time is money". The sign of a company that has become more commercial and more squeezed for space. These are Innocent's last days in Fruit Towers on the Brackenbury Industrial Estate (I'll miss the joke of Fruit Towers being a one-storey shed) before an Eastertime move to a 6-storey block in Ladbroke Grove.

Richard is as upbeat as ever but it's been an extraordinary three years for Innocent since the previous edition of this book. He claims to feel nervous and excited, with excitement rising and nervousness waning. The way he puts it is this: "The business has its mojo back."

As we talk, it becomes clear that the Innocent narrative of happy growth, that dominated its first ten years, had changed suddenly, almost catastrophically.

"Up till Spring 2008 everything had been going our way. Then we hit a perfect storm. Tropicana (owned by Pepsi) launched aggressively against us. They used the same distribution channels as us – but they did that overnight whereas it had taken eight years' slog for us to build those channels. They reduced our revenue by a third, our market share by a third – and the total market shrank at the same time. Fruit was at its highest price ever with countries like China and India importing fruit for their own consumers. The exchange rate collapsed. We lost more money in one year than we had made previously."

It was grim. Richard talks sadly about the change in Monday meetings, moving from a procession of 'new joiners' to 'new leavers'. There was the possibility of going out of business, the reality of plummeting revenues, redundancies and a deep recession. To hang on to what they had – the core of the business that had grown on the promise of healthy, natural, tasty drinks – they needed help. They needed cash. So they went out to the market seeking investment funds.

On the same day, Lehman Brothers collapsed. And financial institutions started crashing all over the world.

The timing could not have been worse. Serious contingency plans were drawn up that would have involved the closure of Innocent's international businesses (in Europe) and the shedding of half the staff. The mission to become the 'earth's favourite little food and drinks company' would have shifted emphasis onto the little. Although the more draconian decisions were avoided it was still, in Richard's words, 'a severe period of retrenchment'.

The fundraising drive had been set in motion. Despite the uncertain financial situation, several offers came in. The expectation of the Innocent founders was that another private investor might be found, someone in the mould of Maurice Pinto, their original business angel. There were some private offers, but they accentuated the uniqueness of Maurice. Other bigger businesses put in bids. One wanted to strip away the requirement to donate 10% of profits to charity. Another demanded business control in return for a majority stake. These were not unusual, outrageous offers in the business world, but Innocent rejected them. It would have gone against their business and brand principles.

The surprising possibility emerged that Coca-Cola might be the one, the real thing. From the first dealings, Coke had been 'completely honest'. They were interested in Innocent because they liked the brand, and they valued its philosophy. They recognised that these were crucial to Innocent's success, and so were the three founders. It was a flattering message to hear – 'We think you're the best people to run the business' – but it also seemed genuine. Certainly, from a commercial viewpoint, it was realistic. Innocent's recent troubles were not of their own making, and the people who had achieved growth for ten years would be the best people to achieve growth for the next ten years.

The negotiations were headed by James Quincey, head of Coca-Cola in the UK and north-western Europe.

The Innocent founders got on with him and other Coke negotiators, finding them straight and straight-talking. So they edged towards a deal.

Richard admits that Innocent were 'cheeky'. He, Adam and Jon made demands that would have tested the patience of other corporations. They were determined to retain control of the business and to have a mechanism inserted in the legal agreement. They asked for, and got, the following. An Investor Board meets quarterly to decide the direction of the business. The Board has four named members: Richard Reed (chairman), Adam Balon, Jon Wright and James Quincey. Decisions are taken by the majority of the Board, so Coca-Cola is outnumbered three-to-one. James Quincey's role is linked to him personally rather than to his role in Coca-Cola. So, as long as Richard, Adam and Jon remain at Innocent and as long as they continue to agree (and remain friends), the control of Innocent remains firmly with the founders.

Another interesting aspect of the deal is that Coca-Cola agreed to support Innocent and not to launch any other juice products in Europe. This is an enormous statement of faith in the Innocent brand. It comes from a history of Coke not having succeeded in Europe with juices. They had launched Minute Maid, but that had not worked in the main markets. Pepsi had succeeded with Tropicana. For Coke, investing in Innocent was the best way to sell juices in the European market. So their words to Innocent were "Let us know what we can do to help".

It all sounds too good to be true, and I say so to Richard. He confesses that there is a part of him that is sad. It's nothing to do with Coke – "they've been great" – but the feeling that it's now unlikely that he'll hand over the keys to his grandchildren. "But that was never part of the vision" he says and shakes himself out of sentimentality to make clear he's pleased with where Innocent has got to. He's an optimist through and through.

"We're still in control. Coke came in first to buy 18% then increased their share to 58%. That gave us the money to do all the things we needed to do, including allowing Maurice Pinto to make his exit. The extra stake changed nothing but it was legally locked down. So, for as long as we wish – perhaps thirty years – Jon, Adam and I run the business as the same Innocent brand with the same philosophy."

"The Coke investment allows us to become a bigger and better version of Innocent. Without it, Innocent would have been a smaller, weaker business. But without Maurice Pinto there would have been no Innocent at all. It was his money and belief, his integrity in sticking to his personal promise when others pulled out, that brought Innocent into the world. So I'm pleased that he's able, at the age of 75, to take his 330 million and use it for the things he loves, like art and ballet."

The conversation has turned emotional. I admire that when so many in the corporate world look away embarrassed at the first sniff of emotion. It also helps to explain why Innocent loyalists stick by the brand. Innocent shows the qualities you like in a good friend but rarely see in a business. Of course, this leads to emotional extremes. The McDonald's furore, three years earlier, had prepared the business for vitriol, as I've described in a previous section of this book.

Richard agrees that the uproar over McDonald's was ten times worse than anything Innocent had to suffer over the Coke deal. He still can't quite understand it.

"It seems a form of corporate racism. It was so

personal to McDonald's. After all, we've always sold our drinks to big businesses – Dunkin' Donuts, Starbucks, Tesco – but they aroused no animosity. With McDonald's it seems like prejudice. But we decided it was better to do what's right not just what sounds right. We certainly didn't take the decision lightly, but you have to ask: Would it be the moral thing to say No? One journalist said to us: "The people who go to McDonald's don't deserve your smoothies". We reject that. It's better to sell healthy drinks to a company that's criticised for selling unhealthy ones. It should be fruit for all, not fruit for west London."

The passion comes from belief in what Innocent does, but is also a reaction to extreme criticism. At the time of the McDonald's kerfuffle, Richard was likened to a 'paedophile' by one 'customer'. With the Coke deal he received death wishes, with one person hoping he would 'get a brain tumour like Anita Roddick'. Such mindless hatred is all the harder to take if you are innocent by name and nature.

But he's always ready to move on, an eternal optimist and a believer in the basic humanity of all the people he deals with. To shift the focus from feelings, we talk about figures. It seems the return of the business mojo is reflected in all sorts of evidence. Sales revenue up. Profits up. Employee engagement up. Customer loyalty up. He recites the sales figures for the last four years, and they tell a story. 2007/£115m; 2008/£105m; 2009/£113m; 2010/£130m. The target for 2011 is £160m, which will mean sales increasing tenfold in ten years. This is success for Innocent, supported by Coca-Cola. The role of invisible supporting partner might not fit with our preconceptions, but the evidence all around Fruit Towers points that way. I always look to one person

181

in particular as the keeper of the Innocent soul: Dan Germain. As creative head, he's the one who nurtures and develops the brand. If there were any backsliding, Dan would know.

Dan doesn't change. Sometimes his beard gets a little longer, but he remains as relaxed and easy to talk to as he's ever been. Asked what he's learnt from the reactions to McDonald's and Coke, he tells me: "How to deal with angry people." For him the Coke deal has meant a bigger creative team in Innocent, and the opportunity to do more of what he loves doing: more products, more packs, more advertising, more social media. The latter is a big change between the previous edition and this one. When we had talked about Innocent in 2008, facebook and twitter had not figured in our conversation.

Conversation is the word Dan always returns to. It's partly because he's so good at it. He describes the era of social media as having a conversation in a new place with new people. It's a reminder too that Dan is the walking, talking embodiment of Innocent's tone of voice. And, for me, through every twist and turn in the Innocent story, its constant strength has been its tone of voice.

Dan is a words man but, as creative head, he has designers in his team. When I ask if the words on packaging are now less important, often replaced by illustrations, he explains that he could never really draw. So when he had fewer people to help creatively, they had to use words because he could write. It's true, of course, but I wonder if a little of the charm has gone out of the Innocent language. When I first came across Innocent it was words on bottles that mattered most, now it seems to be advertising (especially on TV).

"If you want to sell more stuff, you have to do

traditional advertising. Press, posters, TV. The Coke money has helped us expand, in geography and numbers, but we keep exactly the same values. If I draw you a 'pyramid of power', I'd still put bottles at the top, the pinnacle of achievement, with cartons in the middle layer, and advertising at the bottom. But when you're advertising orange juice, our new product, we have to reach new customers. You have to be single-minded. We have naturally wandering minds here, we get sucked into strange places when writing copy for bottles, but you can't wander in a TV ad."

That seems a shame. Dan thinks perhaps it's new territory for Innocent. "Look at the early labels on bottles," he says. "The tone was a bit nervous, we didn't really know what we were doing." Now, with the creative process, he seems very sure about what Innocent is doing.

"Writing for bottles is different now. I used to stay at home one day a week to write a new set of 90 words per label. Now it's two or three people working together on each. We still make it a fun day. We use post-its to put up ideas, then bundle them into thoughts and themes, sketching a story, building from a line. We have a vote to get to the favourites that can then be worked on, either by the designers, or by Ceri to give it some word love. We use the same sort of process for the big packs, kids' juice, Veg Pots, new products."

There have been new products recently and you sense that there will be more to come. Richard had talked about consolidating geographically but dialling up innovation over the next five years. The first signs of this, helped by the Coke investment, are the Veg Pots and Orange/Apple juice in carafes. They're both signs of development while sticking firmly to Innocent's

Piri Piri Veg Pot – one of Innocent's healthy new food products.

The caped crusader adverts, 2010.

principles of healthy, natural food as the basis for everything they produce. Money previously spent on events like Fruitstock – which was much loved but lost Innocent half a million a year – is now spent on product innovation and advertising. Dan even has a pot of 'Be innocent' money for special projects.

The Veg Pots ("it was just the first name and we stuck with it") are the bigger innovation. Using vegetables is a natural sidestep from smoothies made from fruit – but Veg Pots are Innocent's first food products, as distinct from drinks. Veg Pots were launched with four varieties, such as Moroccan squash tagine with giant couscous and fresh coriander. Not surprisingly they are made of vegetables and they come in 400g pots. They make a tasty and healthy lunch, containing three portions of veg, so if you drink an Innocent smoothie while eating a Veg Pot, you hit that five-a-day target with one light meal.

The new Orange/Apple juice carafes are closer to Innocent's original territory. In fact, Innocent has sold orange juice in bottles before without anyone noticing much. But orange juice represents an enormous market, it's a more mainstream product than smoothies (where Innocent are now Europe's established Number 1). It seems that people drink volumes of orange juice at breakfast time while regarding smoothies as a treat at other times of day. So Innocent decided to launch its own juices, in recyclable PET carafes that stand out in supermarkets. The early signs are that the juices will do well. The initial problems are simply to do with being able to make enough to meet demand.

Advertising works. At least it does when you're trying to step up a level to become the name that everyone in Europe associates with fruit juice. Dan Germain likes working with ad agencies, including the current one

Rainey Kelly, because "they know things we don't know". He thinks past Innocent advertising has been too quiet. The development is partly expressed by Dan's voiceover giving way to people like Brian Blessed. A big booming voice helps get your product noticed, but so does the creative idea. Innocent had fun with the 'caped crusader bottle' that appeared in advertising. It fitted Innocent's view of the world, a healthy drink to save you from too many fattening biscuits.

"To be honest, it's also about trying to keep it interesting for us. If we're bored, our consumers will be too. That's where social media have been important. I started blogging, mainly read by London media types, most of whom I never met. I didn't tell anyone, then Rich said we should start an Innocent blog. Well, there was one I'd already prepared, establishing the tone, putting in nonsense and trivia. There was no strategising or theorising, it just happened naturally. It's been the same with facebook and twitter. It's all about making conversation. I get wound up when people parcel it all up as digital strategy. It's just different windows to talk through, a new garden fence to have a chat across."

It pleases Dan to see people around him who so clearly 'get it'. Ceri Tallett now writes more of the words than Dan, and she was behind Innocent's first D&AD Yellow Pencil for best in 'Writing for design' 2010. There's a French marketing director, Thomas de la Brière, who's quickly won everyone's respect. It amuses Dan that Thomas's first British marketing job was with Daddy's Sauce, quintessentially English, and one of his wheezes was to sponsor snooker star Jimmy White to play a tournament as Jimmy Brown. There are now other people who 'have the voice', it's not just Dan and the founders.

Orange juice carafes, launched in 2011.

Other entrepreneurial businesses still look to Innocent for advice and inspiration, so I asked Richard to sum the lessons he draws from Innocent's success. Generosity is a brand value, so here are Richard's thoughts.

1   Get the right brain stuff first

Innocent has always been guided by a set of values. There's a clear sense of purpose. People can connect easily with that. Members of the team feel they're part of something bigger, so do the people who buy Innocent drinks. It's hugely important to have a philosophy and vision, and to stick to them. You need to express all this in the right words, words that people enjoy and relate to. It's like Walmart saying "We give ordinary folk the opportunity to have the same things as rich people."

2   Look after the left brain stuff too

You have to get the economic structure of the business right. People always told Innocent that you need to make a 40% gross margin. In 2008 that slipped to 30% and the company could have gone out of business. If Innocent had minded the economic parameters better, the dip would have been less, the response quicker. Soft hippy stuff is useless unless you get the structure right. Stick to what you know, and concentrate on areas where you can add most value. Innocent decided to concentrate on its brand rather than on running a factory. They buy their own fruit, develop their own products, so they own the intellectual property.

3   It's all about people

It sounds trite but it remains true. Innocent's best and worst decisions have been about recruitment of people. New people come in, you have to work hard to integrate. Sometimes you get it completely wrong. But keeping people engaged and happy is where most of the effort goes.

I leave Fruit Towers in Shepherd's Bush for the last time. My next Innocent visit will be to six storeys of a block in Ladbroke Grove, a new Fruit Towers looking down on the little box where Innocent started. The first and the next offices are just 100 metres apart, but an awful lot of stories in between. People will be sad to go but excited to move on. With Innocent it's always a matter of finding the upside.

About the Author

John Simmons is a writer, trainer and consultant for brands. Until 2003 he was a director of Interbrand, where he established the branding discipline of verbal identity.

Now a director of The Writer *www.thewriter.com* and an independent consultant, John has written many books. His books on the role of language in business communication – from *We, Me, Them & It* through to *Room 121* – have made him the leading and most readable authority in the field.

He was series editor of *Great Brand Stories*, and his books on Starbucks, the Arsenal and Innocent are key titles in the series.

He trains people in more creative business writing through D&AD, The Writer and the Dark Angels programme *www.dark-angels.org.uk* (named after one of his books). He's a regular speaker at conferences and seminars.

His first work of fiction *The Angel of the Stories* was published in 2011 *www.darkangelspress.com*.

OTHER GREAT BRAND STORIES

ARSENAL *Winning Together: The story of the Arsenal brand* by John Simmons & Matt Simmons

BECKHAM *Brand it like Beckham: The Story of How Brand Beckham was Built* by Andy Milligan

DYSON *The Domestic Engineer: How Dyson changed the meaning of cleaning* by Iain Carruthers

eBAY *The Story of a Brand that Taught Millions of People to Trust One Another* by Elen Lewis

GOOGLE *Search Me: The surprising success of Google* by Neil Taylor

GUINNESS *Guinness is Guinness: The colourful story of a black and white brand* by Mark Griffiths

IKEA *Great Ikea! A Brand for All the People* by Elen Lewis

PUMA *The Puma Story: The remarkable turnaround of an endangered species into one of the world hottest sportlifestyle brands* by Rolf-Herbert Peters

STARBUCKS *My Sister's a Barista: How they made Starbucks a home away from home* by John Simmons

UNITED STATES *Brand America: The mother of all brands* by Simon Anholt & Jeremy Kourdi